MW00649565

TH

HARVEST

WAY

1.0

The Green Industry guide for:

Helping you get from where you are now to where you deserve to be... *The Harvest Way*

Ed Laflamme & Bill Arman

Head Harvesters

Editor: Melodee Ann Claassen
Design & Layout: Alissa Johnson
Cover Illustration: Luca Luppi & Alissa Johnson

Address all correspondence to:
Ed Laflamme
284 New Canaan Road
Wilton, CT 06897
Email Address: Ed@harvestlandscapeconsulting.com
Phone: (203) 858-4696

Library of Congress Control Number: Pending
ISBN: 978-0-9911281-2-9

Contents

Introduction

I remember like it was yesterday. My partner, Bill, and I were sitting in the kitchen of his beautiful California home tired from a very long day. We were working on the material for our new Harvest Way Academy. We were creating an internet site that would teach every aspect of the business of landscaping. He poured us a glass of some great cabernet and, after sitting in silence for a minute or so, I remember saying to him, "I bet landscapers would never believe how hard we are working to educate them, to help them really be successful." He agreed. I then added, "You know, the information we are putting in our Academy can make an average landscaper a millionaire if they just read and apply it." At that time each of us had 30+ years of experience in the business and I had been consulting and coaching owners for over 10 years and Bill for about five. We poured our hearts into creating a simple yet complete work that included both video and downloadable guidebooks. We both felt this endeavor was a work of love, a payback as it were, for how successful we had both been in the landscaping business.

Some years have passed since then but we still feel the same way and so do the other Harvesters. We love what we do because we are helping people and, because we are here to help you, we decided to write this book.

You see every organization - its people, customers and leaders - have a heck-of-a-lot more potential than they ever imagined, and we're here to help you "harvest it".

We are here to help you navigate how to get from "here" to "there" easier, faster, and with less pain and mistakes than we had to make. And believe us - with a combined total of over 160 years' experience in the landscape industry - we've made plenty, so we have ample experience to draw on!

Think of this book as a road map that will help you, as the leader of an organization, reach goals that might currently seem unattainable.

Have you ever wondered:

- Is there a better way of doing this?
- Will I ever get to 'there'? (Heck, I'm not even really sure where 'there' is!)
- Is there a 'Road Map' or a better way to get to my Desired Destiny?
- Why does it seem so hard to get to the next level?
- How do I get unstuck and move forward?
- I'm working my pants off and I'm not making any money. Is this effort worth it?
- I keep working 'in my business'. How do I figure out how to work 'on it'?
- How can I get help and guidance?

Well, in this book we try to do the best we can to give you the answers to these questions. We try to offer a simple step-by-step process that builds upon itself, one piece at a time.

To guide you in this journey, we've provided the fundamental thinking and actions to systematically lead you and your team to become, "best in class".

Once there, you can fully "Harvest Your Potential" and also "Harvest The Profits"!

HOW TO USE THIS BOOK

Whenever we (The Harvesters) read a book, we usually go through it looking for key takeaways and areas that apply to our current needs. We're on the hunt for quotes that "ring a bell" or for actionable items that will help us become better leaders, speakers, or Harvesters. So we wrote this book with that philosophy in mind, making it easy to flip through and find the section you're looking for, including some action steps and bits of knowledge that can help you start improving your business today.

LEARN THE COMMON ROADBLOCKS AND OBSTACLES

You'll save time, heartache, and money if you can learn the common roadblocks and obstacles others have faced, and the way to overcome them. It's our hope that our experience will help you avoid some obstacles entirely, or prepare you to deal with them whenever they might arise, so they do not stop you on your path to success.

TAKE ACTION

Harvester Ed says, "Nothing happens unless YOU, make it happen, if YOU don't make it happen, nothing will happen for YOU!"

It's nice to read a book and feel good about yourself and your organization, but these "feelings" can quickly get waylaid as the fast and furious daily business challenges take over. If a line or section jumps out at you, don't just nod along, pick up a pen or highlighter and mark it up, write notes, underline, whatever - that's why we wrote it, to give you ideas, to study it, and try new things. It's up to you to be diligent about converting the ideas, recommendations, suggestions, tricks, tips, tactics, traits, and "best practices" we review in this book into action items for you to build upon.

Harvester Backgrounds

BILL:

The Harvest Group started with a vision. Well, that, and a few glasses of red wine while Ed and I mulled over walls covered with flip charts of our plans and dreams mapping out what we could do with the combined knowledge we had accrued during our decades of working in the landscape industry. Ed got his experience and put in his time on the east coast, while I got my experience and put in my time on the west. Together, we had a clear scope of all aspects of the business whether they were really BIG or really small and knew how things worked.

ED:

That's true. While Bill put in his time working with ValleyCrest on the West Coast, I was in Connecticut building my landscaping business in the East. I started my company in 1971 with $700 that I borrowed from my mother to buy out my then partner. I had just finished the first season servicing clients, working out of the back of the trunk of my car. Nine years later, I sold the residential segment of the business for exponentially more than the seed money I had started it with and concentrated my energies on the commercial and industrial sectors. A few years after that shift, in 1985, I was awarded the GE World Headquarters contract in Fairfield, CT, followed by nine more world corporate headquarter contracts, making my company the largest landscape maintenance contractor in the state. In 1998, Laflamme Services, Inc. was listed as one of the top 100 revenue-generating landscaping companies in America by *Lawn & Landscape* magazine and was voted in the top 25 best landscape companies in America.

I relate these achievements and awards as a way to attest that when it comes to landscaping, I have seen a great deal. But, before going any further, I attribute my company's success to the incredibly great people that I worked with. As the years passed while owning my company I came to realize, "we are not really in the landscaping business but in the people business doing landscaping".

A year after being featured by *Lawn & Landscape* I sold my company to Landcare USA, and shortly thereafter joined Bill, starting my new career as a landscape business consultant.

It's been 45 years in this industry now, and I still look forward to every day. I love what I do and I love helping landscapers Harvest Their Potential! It's been a personally rewarding journey in that I have had the opportunity to not just help companies grow and improve their profits but, as a result, change people's lives!

BILL:

While Ed was working on the East Coast I spent nearly 30 years working at America's largest privately held family-owned landscape firm, ValleyCrest Companies. After graduating from Cal Poly - San Luis Obispo with a BS in Ornamental Horticulture, I started my illustrious career at the bottom (and I mean the very bottom, dispersing the grass that sticks together when it's wet, commonly known as "turf turds"!) and worked my way through every field position and then on to sales, and then to management positions. I climbed my way to the top, eventually holding the position of Regional Vice President of the Southern California Region, overseeing a $25 Million portfolio in six branch offices and five service lines . . . not to mention my other position later on as the VP of Human Resources, overseeing the operations of nearly 6,500 employees - so, yeah, you could say I've seen my share of the industry, too!

Ed and I know how fickle and frustrating this business can be.

We felt strongly that there were a lot of companies out there, looking for a better way to run their businesses. We had seen it from the trenches - a whole bunch of folks struggling just as much as we had, all running into the same sorts of obstacles that could have easily been avoided with a little guidance.

In the summer of 2007, the Harvest Group was officially launched - and since then our lives, and the lives of our clients, have never been the same.

ED:

We formed the foundations and principles for the Harvest Group from the mindshare projects we've been involved in since we began working together advising clients in 2007.

Since then we've held workshops, written articles for leading publications, and been featured as speakers for organizations such as NALP (National Association of Landscape Professionals) and state and national landscape conferences.

I wrote a book on the business of landscaping titled *"Green Side Up"* and Bill has written one titled *"The Harvest Way for Recruiting and Hiring the Right People"*. We've built instruction kits and created FREE Harvest Group weekly video instructionals that can be found on our website, HarvestLandscapeConsulting.com. Our instructional 3-minute weekly videos reach over 10,000 industry leaders who tune in each week to watch, laugh, and learn.

BILL:

As with all the content we've created and the classes we've run, you'll see in this book we are fond of offering simple steps and practical ways for organizations to improve, one step at a time. If you like the golden nuggets of knowledge you find in here, check out our online learning center at the HarvestWayAcademy.com to get access to more tools, downloadable guide books, videos, and online classes.

We promise you'll gain a landscape business education unlike any you've ever found. And, like both of us, you'll be able to "Harvest Your Potential" and see your business grow!

Today, The Harvest Group has grown to include 4 additional Harvesters:

Steve Cesare has a Ph.D. in Industrial/Organizational Psychology & more than 25 years of human resources experience with Bemus Landscape, Jack in the Box, & NASA.

Cindy Code is an award-winning journalist who spent 22 years with *Lawn & Landscape* magazine communicating with contractors nationwide in her roles as editor, account manager, publisher and Internet content manager. She earned a reputation as a respected journalist, communicator and active participant within the industry.

Fred Haskett, who has wide Green Industry experience. During his 40+ year career, Fred has been both an Owner and Senior Leader with The Brickman Group, ValleyCrest and U.S. Lawns. He has a background in Lawn Care, Tree Care, Landscape Maintenance, and Snow Service.

Alison A Hoffmann has more than 25 years of experience in strategy, operations, mergers and acquisitions and delivering business-to-business client solutions. Her areas of expertise include managing operations for profitable growth, organizational design and strategy activation.

The Buckets

Some 25 years ago, when we were trying to figure out the best way to logically divide up a company, we discovered there were really 8 distinct parts. We affectionately called them "the 8 buckets". What follows are the 8 buckets along with the appropriate stepping stones under each. By using these buckets you will better understand your company and be able to figure out where you are strong and where you need work.

Study carefully each of these "buckets" and the "stepping stones" because they contain the foundational principles for success in the landscaping business. For further information on these visit our online learning center called, The Harvest Way Academy mentioned above.

BUCKET #1:
CULTURE

In the first 20 minutes after walking into a company, we can feel if there's a positive or negative environment, if there's tension or if it's a cool place to be.

This sort of atmosphere is created by your company culture - a system of informal and formal rules that define how people will behave and feel about your company.

It comes as no surprise that companies with strong cultures out-perform those with weak ones. A strong culture helps align employees so they view the sum of all their efforts as greater than their individual parts. It keeps people working together, rather than alongside or against one another, and inspires employees to put more care and effort into their work.

Likewise, companies with weak cultures painfully exist. Either employees trudge around and perform at the lowest acceptable level to avoid getting fired or they excel at their job and quickly move on in order to find a more enjoyable work environment.

It's not hard to guess which will yield a greater profit - and the first step to building a strong company culture starts with you.

STEPPING STONE 1: LEADER'S ROLE

Every company has a culture, but whether it's consciously developed or not is up to you, the owner.

It's worth it to take courses and read books on leadership and charisma if you haven't already. Sure, you might be a good worker and great in the field but, as the owner of a company, you need to be more than just that, you need to learn how to command and inspire.

When it comes to influencing your company's culture, you set the tone, you set the pace, and you control how your culture will hinder or help your business.

STEPPING STONE 2: DEFINE EXISTING CULTURE

Let's take a quick reality check.

Write down good and bad words describing your company culture. Now, without revealing what you wrote, have some key managers and employees do the same. The matching words will reveal the true nature of your company culture.

With most companies we help, we've found the word list is all over the place. This is usually because the company's core VISION, MISSION, and VALUES are either non-existent or need work.

STEPPING STONE 3: DEFINE/BUILD DESIRED CULTURE

A VISION

Gives shape to the future of an organization and inspires people to be greater together by working towards an ultimate goal.

A MISSION

Is a company's purpose that will lead to the realization of its vision.

VALUES

Are what a company and its workforce cherish and honor.

We have plenty of Harvest Way workshops and tools that focus on developing these three building blocks of a company's culture, setting the rules for what type of behavior should be rewarded, expected, and banned.

For example, if your company's VISION is to be renowned as "the landscaping experts", your MISSION should be to have a workforce of educated employees. A clear way to pursue this MISSION is by placing a cultural VALUE on education by hiring people based on their ability and desire to learn and providing them with opportunities to further their knowledge. Such actions will encourage a company-wide behavior that successfully contributes to that culture of landscape expertise.

> **ACTION STEP:** Set aside time with your core team to build and write your core VISION, MISSION, and VALUES.

STEPPING STONE 4: ONBOARDING

A strong company culture will help:

- Guide a hiring process. Look to hire employees that are a good fit and share similar values and passions.
- Create clear goals and expectations. Employees and managers will have a better sense of what actions will be rewarded and those which will be frowned upon.
- Develop relevant and more specific learning programs for your employees to improve themselves.
- Differentiate you from competitors.
- Improve customer relations.
- Encourage loyalty and a sense of companionship.
- Inspire innovation.

As with every construction site, there are hazards to avoid while building, the same, too, with your company culture - or as we call them, "culture busters".

Culture busters are people within your company that detract from its VISION. These are the employees that are the gossip mongers and the ones that can't seem to get on board with whatever your core VALUES might be.

Cut loose the slack and hire people who fit with your company culture.

STEPPING STONE 5: TRAINING AND REVIEWS

Once you've defined your core VISION, MISSION, and VALUES, align your employees with these cultural building blocks so they can function as a team.

Accomplish this by creating bonding rituals like celebrating the first day of rain, providing seminars and programs that are relevant to a skillset you want all your employees to exhibit, or by giving recognition to employees who are star examples of embodying a cultural trait.

There are plenty of books and professionals you can use to help get you on the right track. You can find more culture-building tools and details related to the landscaping industry at the Harvest Way Academy.

Whatever it is you do - from hiring, to taking on new projects, to creating company-sponsored events - make sure you ask and can answer the one simple question:

How does this shape the culture of the company?

> **ACTION STEP:** Create bonding rituals that reinforce your company culture.

CULTURE EXERCISE

After you have finished reading this section, take some time to stop and take a good look at this critical area of your business. It has been proven that the most successful companies in the world have great cultures and are considered to be "Healthy Organizations".

Earlier, we mentioned that you and your team should take some time and ask yourselves a few questions.

Here are several you should consider. Ask yourselves -

- Do you have your Vision, Mission, and Core Values spelled out in writing?
- What is your Vision Statement? (This should Inspire to Aspire and even to Perspire!)

Write your Vision Statement here:

_____

What is your Mission? (Your Company's Purpose; If each and every person did this every day, the organization would reach its Vision)

_____

What are your Core Values? (4-5 Key Values – Values that you stand for and that are non-negotiable)

_____

- Does every employee have a copy of these and fully embrace them starting at the top? If not, why? What needs to be done to remedy this?
- Are these part of your onboarding program with new team members? How will you make this happen?
- Are they part of your performance review process? Add this to your review process and hold people accountable.
- If you do have them, can each leader either write them down without looking them up or verbally affirm them? If not, why not?
- If you do not have these in place, the Harvesters highly recommend that you build these together as a team. You may even want to have an outside facilitator help you and your team to build these. This usually takes 4-8 hours to build.

This exercise alone will help build a positive and healthy culture.

Remember that this important area of your business starts with the leader.

"People hear your words but they believe your behavior."
Mark Sanborn

We also encourage you to take the Culture Quiz, a 10-question culture check-up that will help you recognize where you stand with your culture. The Culture Quiz, along with an entire culture building program, can be found in our Harvest Way Academy. It's called "Got Culture? Get Culture!". In this part of the Academy, Harvesters Bill and Ed walk you and your organization through ways to build your culture with our video and guidebook.

One thing the Harvesters know for certain is that all great "Leaders are Readers" so, with that said, you will find some reading assignments along our journey together in this book.

Highly Recommended Reading Assignment (This is a must read for all of the leaders in your organization.)

The Advantage: Why Organizational Health Trumps Everything Else in Business by Patrick Lencioni

Harvester Tip: One way to have your organization become a continually learning organization is to read! We suggest that your team read together, as a team, AT LEAST one great book per month. Make some time to review your learning from the book and see how it can help build your team and its culture.

BUCKET #2:
PEOPLE

So, you thought you were in the landscape business?

Think again!

In reality, you're in the people business, doing landscaping. Your People (your team) are one of the most critical parts to your success.

Wheelbarrows, shovels, and rakes are just plastic, metal, and wood without people who know how to use them; but, get the right team on board, and you can build an empire.

The companies that are the best with people will be the best companies. It is that simple and that important.

Your company's ability to find, attract, get on board, keep, and grow the right people will be its greatest challenge and at the root of its success or failure.

STEPPING STONE 1: CULTURE AND COMPLIANCE

On the road to success, "Culture" is the car you drive and "Compliance" is being a competent enough driver so you don't get pulled over or crash along the way.

Having a clear understanding of your company's identity, core values, strengths, and weaknesses will help you attract the right people so you don't waste time on duds.

Make sure your handbook, company policies, and employment practices are within the bounds of the law because this will save you from fines, lawsuits, and other legal hazards that you could encounter on the road in the "People Business" of landscaping.

CULTURE

Every company has a Culture whether that company is aware of it or not. A company that spends time nurturing its culture will have an identity that both its customers and employees can readily recognize and understand.

A well-defined company culture helps builds a solid recruiting and retention program, provides a sense of destiny and purpose, and shapes how people align and work together.

Likewise, companies that lack a defined culture will grow one haphazardly, usually resulting in employees being self-serving, working without a larger sense of purpose, and performing at the lowest acceptable level to avoid termination.

GET CULTURE

To build your company's culture, there are three categories every company leader should be able to answer:

1) What is the company's Vision?

2) What is the company's Mission?

3) What are the company's Core Values?

If you are unsure about these answers and would like to learn more about what they stand for and how to discover them, check out our *"Got Culture? Get Culture!: Build & Shape a Great Culture"* guidebook at Harvestwayacademy.com/the-8-buckets/courses/.

> **ACTION STEP:** Build and write out your company's Vision, Mission, and Core Values.

HIRE RIGHT

Don't just hire to fit the job, hire to fit the culture. Company culture should act as a compass when it comes to deciding who is the right candidate.

Culture starts at the top, with you, and trickles down through your chain of command. The higher up someone is with your company, the more influential they are in affecting its culture.

>**ACTION STEP:** Make a list of "Must Haves" and "Would Like to Haves" in an employee and then build interview questions that address the desired traits.

CULTURE CATALYSTS

As your company evolves its core values, find opportunities to make them stronger. Employee events and scheduled team gatherings are some examples of how you can do this. To see others and get detailed worksheets on improving your culture, check out Harvestwayacademy.com/the-8-buckets/courses/.

COMPLIANCE

Now that everyone is behaving well and aligning with your company's culture, is everything within the bounds of the law?

When it comes to running a company that deals with people on a large scale, it's not a matter of if you will be sued, it's a matter of when.

Following are the most common potholes and some ways you can avoid totaling your company if you run into one:

HR ASSESSMENTS

Every employee you hire is a potential lawsuit. In order to avoid such legal hazards, it's important to conduct an HR Assessment at least once a year.

An HR assessment should rate the major human resources programs in your company on a 1-5 star-scale (i.e. staffing, training, performance management, compensation practices, etc.).

Is each program:

- Fair?
- Legal?
- Aligned with business objectives?
- Make it a priority to fix whichever of your programs scored the lowest.

Search for our Harvest Way HR Assessment Sheet in our Academy to get a more detailed idea of what to look for.

> **ACTION STEP:** Conduct an HR Assessment at least annually and evaluate points of vulnerability and potential risks to your company.

EXTERNAL

If your company does not comply with all the local, state and federal laws, guidelines, and regulations, it risks encountering financial penalties that can cripple your operations. While we know these things are always changing, you can cover your bases by focusing on the most common areas a company will usually get audited or fined for. You can find a detailed list on our website.

INTERNAL

When it comes to the nitty-gritty of Human Resources, there's usually so much clutter and mountains of documents that it's hard to keep everything organized. Make your life easier by simplifying your Human Resources program.

> **ACTION STEP:** Audit your key HR procedures and see if you can make them simpler.

SAFETY PROGRAM

Make sure you have a safety program in place that everyone on the ladder, from your employees to your executives, participates in.

A good safety program will maintain OSHA compliance and should have:

- Annual safety goals;
- Up-to-date tailgate safety training;
- A high-quality PPE;
- A strong Medical Provider Network – an entity or group of health care providers to treat injured workers on the job; and,
- A way to track and monitor your company's safety culture.

I-9 FORMS

You can be fined up to $1100 per error on each I-9 Form you fill out for your employees, so you'd better make sure you're doing these right.

Make it a part of your company culture to audit this part of your HR department annually to make sure your I-9 documents are accurate and up-to-date.

POSTERS AND POLICY MODIFICATIONS

Legally required posters about employment and legal standards should be posted in all locations by the early part of January each year.

BIGGEST MISTAKES

Discrimination – This is where your company will be most vulnerable to the people it hires. Avoid this pitfall by conducting an annual review of your HR processes, train managers and supervisors on relevant EEO issues, and keep your newsfeed up-to-date with ongoing changes to state and federal employment laws.

Fair Labor Standards Act – Keep accurate wage and hour records that are in line with the Fair Labor Standards Act.

Common offenses include:

- Working non-exempt employees off the clock
- Paying employees cash instead of payroll checks
- Not paying proper overtime wages

<u>OSHA</u> – There are a ton of OSHA regulations and the average fine is $2,300 per violation. Over 70% of OSHA inspections are unannounced. So it's worthwhile to make sure both you and your HR are current with the most common OSHA guidelines.

> **ACTION STEP:** Make room for one day a year where you self audit your HR program and make sure it's up to date with: I-9, OSHA, Safety Program, Posters, Wage, and Employment Records.

STEPPING STONE 2: HR ADMINISTRATION

Sometimes equipment breaks and plants won't grow - but weed-whackers and geraniums won't sue you, people will.

The people that work for you can be your greatest asset and they can be your greatest liability.

Not having clear written policies on how to deal with Human Resource issues before they arise is like planting seeds without weeding. You will leave yourself open to the risk of lawsuits and fines by internal and external sources.

The best tactic is to have a HR consultant on hand to keep you out of trouble when making key decisions, such as hiring or firing someone. If this is not an option, you can cover most of your bases by making sure these four fundamentals are in order:

1) COMPANY HANDBOOK & POLICY

Have an attorney that specializes in Labor Law review the Handbook and Policies. Make sure updates and revisions are made and distributed every January and to all new hires on their first day of work.

2) JOB DESCRIPTIONS

This is the foundation of Human Resources. Each position in your company should have a written job description that defines all aspects of the job and is reviewed by a subject-matter-expert each year.

Each employee should receive his/her written job description on his/her first day of work and again during the annual performance review process.

Job descriptions can act as a legal defense against claims of discrimination when it comes to hiring, staffing, training, compensation, and performance evaluation - so make sure they are watertight!

3) PERSONNEL FILES

Make an easily accessible file and keep well-organized work records on each employee. The files should include everything from tax forms to job descriptions, signed waivers, and legally articled procedures and documents wherein an employee acknowledges your company's policies.

4) TIME CARDS

This is not just a job for accounting. Having a daily regimented time card process that includes initializations and no altering will protect you against:

- Federal wage/hour issues
- Leaves of absences (i.e. paid and unpaid, sick days, vacation days, etc.)
- Worker's compensation investigations

Be aware that every state has a different standard when it comes to work week, meal periods, breaks, overtime, and drive time.

> **ACTION STEP:** Review your company Handbook and Policies. Do you have clear Job Descriptions? Are your personnel files organized and easy to access? Are your Time Cards well organized and clear? If not, visit Harvestwayacademy.com/the-8-buckets/courses for help.

STEPPING STONE 3:
ORGANIZATIONAL STRUCTURE

Every ship has a clear-cut chain of command. We find it helps to make a visual diagram of the people and their positions in a 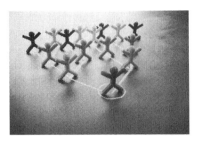 company to get a clearer idea of what that chain actually looks like.

We have examples of these sorts of People Diagrams at the Harvest Way Academy, or you can make your own. Either way, once you've made it, here are a few practical ways you can use it to improve your company:

ID TRAINING AND RECRUITING NEEDS

Now that you have your diagram made, you will be able to get a better idea of the different levels of leadership and organization. Being able to quickly identify who reports to whom and which positions are open and which are occupied, will allow you to optimize your recruiting program by prioritizing which positions need to be filled or replaced. It will also give you an easy way to determine which training programs and developmental skills for your team members are worthwhile to invest in.

RANK TOP PERFORMERS

Assign an A,B,C, etc., ranking to your team members so you can easily sort them by their potential and ability to perform.

This will also expose the weak and strong areas of your company and should help guide your decisions when hiring and firing people.

CAREER LADDER

There's nothing like the clear incentive of a promotion to get people to work harder and remain more loyal to your company.

We like to have our clients project three years forward and build a future People Diagram based on their current revenue stream, where they want their company to be, and the proper way to make it grow.

For more information on building a detailed People Diagram, see Chapter 6, Step 1, of "Recruiting and Hiring the Right People" in the Harvest Way Academy.

STEPPING STONE 4: RECRUITING

In the same way you wouldn't mow a lawn without having a lawn mower, you shouldn't recruit without having some recruiting tools.

While we have a comprehensive kit of recruiting lists and tricks at our Harvest Way Academy, there are a few basic steps you can take to improve your recruiting program today.

YOUR FUNNEL

The most important thing to maintaining a healthy pool of qualified workers is your funnel - or how prospective employees will find their way into your workforce.

1) Hire Internally: Look at this option first as it will give people in your company a chance to advance and will avoid causing disharmony by hiring a new person to be above the old ones.

2) Have Employees Help: Enlist employees to help with the search and offer employees monetary referral bonuses.

3) Vendors: Pick your top vendors and let them know the specifics of what you're looking for.

4) Professional Organizations: Any professional landscape organization you might belong to is a great resource for finding skilled individuals.

5) The Community: If you know where your target worker frequents, get involved in the community by giving talks, writing articles for the local paper, advertising on billboards or the radio, or doing community projects so you can stay visible.

6) Agencies: Temp and placement agencies, like the H2B Visa Program, are a good resource when it comes to having a large number of people in your funnel, but don't depend on these as they're not always reliable.

7) Online: Your website, electronic job boards, and social media outlets.

8) Always Be Looking: Always be on the lookout for good employee candidates and hire the best when they appear.

KNOW WHO YOU'RE LOOKING FOR

When you're recruiting it helps to know who and what you need.

Look at your best and worst employees and write what you like/don't like about them and where you found them.

Now, take stock of the positions you need to fill on your team and write the requirements that are necessary to fill the job.

Some details you might get specific about like age, demographic, education, or certifications will help you identify the areas to advertise to find the best candidate(s), such as schools, churches, parks, etc., and how to entice that person to come work for you.

HAVE A STANDARD INTERVIEW PROCESS

When you finally do get a candidate into the office for an interview, have an extensive list of interview questions, screens to weed out unqualified people, and a ranking system so you can judge each candidate fairly. For ideas related to interview questions, check out Harvestwayacademy.com/the-8-buckets/courses/

While questioning potential new hires about their past experiences, we suggest using the EAR method - ask for an Example, what Action they took, and what were their Results.

At the end of the interview, remember to ask how that person found you. Data from this question will allow you to further hone your recruiting funnel.

> **ACTION STEP:** What is your funnel like? Do you have a pool of qualified candidates in case one of your jobs needs to be filled? If not, try enlisting one of the above-mentioned outlets to expand the size of your funnel.

STEPPING STONE 5: ONBOARDING

You never get a second chance to make a first impression.

Statistics show that new hires with bad feelings about their first few days and weeks at a company will not last.

When a new employee is hired, it's one of the most influential times to shape their perspective about your company. If they feel good about working for you, they will perform better and be more productive. If they feel your company doesn't care for them, then why should they care for it?

It's worth the time, effort, and money on the front end to go the extra mile when it comes to getting your new employees "On Board" with your company.

FIRST DAY

The landscape industry has some work to do when it comes to making a good impression on the first day. The usual process is to have a person fill out paperwork, watch a video, take a drug test, and then it's off to the field. It's all very impersonal, and that's the message it's sending to them about your company. But, imagine how new hires would feel if you also found a moment during their first day to personally welcome them aboard the team.

Where leaders spend their time is perceived as important by the team and, by spending time with individuals on their first day, you're sending the message that you care about your workers.

PREPARE THEM

1) Any tools or uniforms new employees need should be ready on their first day of work.

2) Cover company basics with new hires before they enter the field:

- Arrival
- Safety
- Company Vision/Mission/Values
- Employee Manual
- Legal Paperwork (Equal Opp, Sexual Harassment, FMLA, etc.)

3) Either you or a designated new hire team should host a mini boot camp with two to four hours of training.

KEEP A CLEAR LINE OF COMMUNICATION

1) Identify and review all basic training and work expectations for new hires during their first 90 days.

2) Give and request feedback.

3) Assign a coach/buddy who can help new hires become successful team members.

Check out the 10-15 Report at the Harvest Way Academy for a fast and easy way to touch base with new hires.

> **ACTION STEP:** Ask a recently hired employee what his/her first day/week was like and see where you can improve the "Onboarding" process.

STEPPING STONE 6:
PERFORMANCE MANAGEMENT

The success of an organization depends on how well team members perform. All your employees need to know how they are doing and what is needed for them to achieve success within the organization.

Performance management provides managers and supervisors the ability to set goals and give feedback to team members. It also helps team members understand what they need to improve and what they are doing well.

THREE TYPES OF GOALS

1) S.M.A.R.T. GOALS:

- Specific
- Measurable
- Ambitious and achievable
- Results based
- Time bound

2) DEVELOPMENT GOALS

Goals that focus on skills you want the team member to develop in order to advance in his/her career.

3) PERFORMANCE GOALS

This is a goal that measures how well the team member is working in a specific area and sets a higher standard for him/her to achieve.

RATING PITFALLS

Leniency - Not being consistently strict enough with your rating system will skew results.

Halo Effect - Rating an employee based on a single performance, rather than factoring in the entire review period.

<u>Central Tendency</u> - Not wanting to rate employees high or low, so everyone is clustered in the middle and hard to tell apart.

<u>Impressions</u> - Rating an employee based on impressions and gut feelings, rather than on concrete, observable examples gathered over a period of time.

DISCUSSING PERFORMANCE

This is a great opportunity to build the supervisor-employee partnership:

1) Before the meeting:

- Provide the employee with a copy of his/her evaluation
- Schedule uninterrupted time
- Anticipate possible reactions

2) During the meeting:

- Break the ice
- Review the goals and completed tasks one by one
- Discuss the places the employee is strong, could use improvement, and the overall performance rating
- Address career development opportunities
- Identify at least one DEVELOPMENT GOAL for the coming year
- Redirect the conversation if things get off topic
- Focus on the issue, not the person
- Share the conversation
- Establish clear, measurable agreed-upon objectives
- Work together to create S.M.A.R.T. performance goals

3) Closing the meeting:

- Get employee or supervisor's signature to document the meeting took place
- Document thoughts on the meeting to refer back to in the future

ACTION STEP: Review your PERFORMANCE MANAGEMENT process to see if you're keeping accurate records on all your employees' failures and successes.

STEPPING STONE 7: GROWING THEM

If people don't feel like they're growing, then they're going. People want to learn. If you can turn your company into an organization that helps people grow, then you will have a smarter workforce and higher employee retention.

HOW TO GROW

Take stock of who your employees are to determine what sort of education and growth opportunities you can provide.

For instance, if they're Hispanic workers, maybe they need English lessons or a path to getting a driver's license.

If they're technical workers, look to night courses or seminars to help them improve their skills. You could also encourage them to look for reasonable courses on their own, by offering to cover the cost of education.

Even providing certifications through your company is a way to make your culture into a learning organization.

When you help a person to become better, they will become more valuable to your company and feel more loyal to you.

WHO TO GROW

When picking those special employees to invest extra time and money into, it's best to look at your PEOPLE DIAGRAM to determine who to help:

- How do you rate that person's loyalty?
- What position does that person hold?
- What position would you like him/her to occupy in the future?
- Sometimes you might just have a feeling about a person - in this industry, gut instinct counts for something.

It's worth it to take chances on people that show you they're hard workers and who you believe have a sincere desire to learn and improve themselves. Maybe that person just never got a chance to flourish and, if you're the one to provide them that chance, imagine the mutually beneficial relationship that would build.

NURTURING GROWTH

When you plant a seed, you've got to water it. Start a coaching and mentoring program in your organization. Every new person in your company should have a mentor regardless of his/her position.

The day a new person comes on board there should be a fellow employee whom they can ask questions of and with whom they can discuss problems. Once employees feel more established, link them to a new employee of their own. Such inner rank companionship will make a stronger chain of workers.

When it comes to higher up people like the management team, consider using professional career or business coaches to guide them in becoming better.

> **ACTION STEP**: Find at least one course or class that you can offer your employees to help them grow.

STEPPING STONE 8: ON KEEPING THEM

There's an average 15-20% turnover in the green industry. After investing so much time finding and training the right people, such high turnover can kill you. Luckily, there's something you can do to reduce the number of people that leave your company.

WHY PEOPLE LEAVE & HOW TO FIX IT

- Lack of recognition
  - FIX
    - Recognize people for doing a good job in private and in front of others
    - Be specific about what that person did
    - Spend more time reinforcing positive behavior than condemning for bad behavior

34

- Give awards in the forms of food, money, or bonuses

- Lack of input in making decisions
  - FIX
    - Occasionally ask employees for opinions either one by one, in small groups, or surveys.
    - Ask for suggestions on how to improve certain areas of your company (i.e. customer service, work quality, safety, etc.)
    - Hold occasional "town hall" meetings

- Not being used to their potential
  - FIX
    - Take inventory of your people's talents and see when you can use them
    - Make a wish-list of special projects and put together a task for utilizing people's talents with rewards as incentive
    - Have more skilled employees become part of an advisory team

- Not opportunity for advancement
  - FIX
    - Have a clearly mapped out career ladder for employees, adding more responsibility as they move up
    - Make sure all positions have room for advancement

- Not Challenged
  - FIX
    - Give them more assignments
    - Give them the opportunity to change locations if they want to

- Feeling underpaid
  - FIX
    - Review your compensation packages to see if you're competitive with other companies

- For published pay ranges, see www.landcarenetwork.org
- Make sure their workload/pay wage is balanced

- Boss is a bad leader
  - FIX
    - Perform exit interviews with all employees
    - Conduct annual employee surveys to get input on managers and company
    - Once you're aware someone is a problem, take steps to make improvements

- Broken promises
  - FIX
    - Put all agreements in writing and have both parties sign

- Bad company culture
  - FIX
    - Seek professional advice from HR department or outside consultant
    - Be aware of what your company culture is like

- Overwhelming workload
  - FIX
    - Review projects and bring in more people to help when necessary
    - Take action and identify the issue as soon as you hear about it
    - Seek input from employees if they seem stressed out

KEEP THE KEEPERS

1) Take an honest look at your retention rate and see if your program needs a tune-up. Ask yourself:

- How many people have left your organization in the last 3 years?
- How many were keepers?

2) Have a 3rd party conduct an anonymous survey at least once a year to measure employee morale and see where you need to improve.

3) Stage a company retreat where team members can reflect, plan, and bond.

4) Be honest with yourself about your own performance as a leader:

- Seek professional guidance and advice
- Briefly step away from the reins to gain a better perspective
- Establish an employee advisory board
- Live by your own rules
- Be realistic toward the reasons why good people are leaving and make every effort to get these remedied

  ACTION STEP: Take an honest look at your employee retention rate by making a list of people who have left within the last three years and why.

PEOPLE EXERCISE

Okay, we hope that after reading this bucket you realize how important the role of the RIGHT people plays in the success of your business. In fact, we believe that this ONE BUCKET alone, if mastered by an organization, will almost certainly assure a company to be successful.

And, yes, we know that this is easier said than done.

Remember this -

> *"Having the Right People in the Right Spot Doing the Right Things and Doing the Right Things Right along with treating them Right will get you the RIGHT RESULTS, Right? Right!!!"*
> Harvester Bill

The Harvesters believe the very foundation of a successful organization will have this mantra absolutely ringing in the hearts and minds of everyone on the team.

We must consider this one of our top four priorities as an organization and we must master the following:

"Find, Attract, Get On Board, Keep, and Grow the Right People."
The Harvesters

So, with this in mind, take a look at the assignments we have given you in this section to help you accomplish this one essential piece of a company that will indeed "harvest your potential".

Action Steps: Here are some Key Areas to take action on -

- Draw a "People Map" or Org Chart of where you are now and what you will look like three years from now with People.
- Identify your recruiting needs now and in the future. Build a solid recruiting program.
- Build a Career Ladder. Show the opportunities for advancement for existing and new team members.
- Decide who your A-B-C players are and what needs to be done with each level.
- Define in writing what your culture is all about using a Vision, Mission, and Core Value Statement.
- Have an outside HR professional review your Employee Manual and adjust accordingly.
- Perform an HR Assessment by an outside HR expert to verify you are in compliance.
- Have a very robust Safety Program in place.

BUCKET #3:
CUSTOMERS

In the landscape service industry, customer relationships are the roots of success - but how deep those roots go will determine how well your business will grow and how much fruit it will bear.

Think about it: Do you have a favorite place you go to get a haircut, favorite restaurant to eat, or hotel chain that you swear by?

Such places are more than just the product or service they offer - they keep you coming back because, when you're their customer, you feel good.

ED:

In my hometown of Wilton, Connecticut, there was a failing hardware store that was taken over by a fellow named Matt, who had very little knowledge about the industry. Matt did, however, know about people. One day, while rummaging around the store's cellar, Matt found a vintage popcorn machine. After giving it a hardy scrub and filling it with kernels, he placed the machine near the store's entrance, so that the smell of fresh popcorn was the first thing to greet people as they walked through the door. The popcorn was free, and every time my boys would hear that I was going to the store to pick up an item, they'd ask if they could come along.

It was such a simple, inexpensive thing - free popcorn - and that, along with Matt's gregarious disposition, transformed a normally mundane experience into something exciting. As a direct result of Matt's above-average customer service, the hardware store that was once a failing business, began to thrive.

There are different relationship levels you can achieve with your customers.

At the most basic level you are just another commodity but, as you build more rapport and win customers over with your service and culture, you will gain fiercely loyal supporters, job security, and even generate new business via customers' word of mouth.

Over the years we've learned that the average landscape business only devotes about 2% or less of its revenue to advertising, instead depending on such "word of mouth" as the preferred method to win new business.

Focusing on how customers experience your company directly affects how well it will do.

STEPPING STONE 1: CUSTOMER SELECTION

Find your ideal customer, then do what you can to attract them.

We know that when you're first starting off it might be necessary to take every job to increase cash flow but, as soon as that cash flow is satisfied, create a customer selection criteria that will guide you when to say "no" and when to say "go" after a customer.

In the long run it pays to be picky. It will save you time, make you more money, and keep you producing better quality work because you'll care more about the job. If you try to provide a service for everyone that comes your way, you won't have time to focus on the clients that you really want, and your dream business will remain just that - a dream.

People tend to keep similar company and working with customers you enjoy will usually lead to more referrals with a similar sort of people.

If you don't know what type of customers you want, refer to your company's Vision, Mission, and Values to help steer you in the right direction.

At the Harvest Way Academy, we give members a Customer Selection Criteria form that helps them target their desired core market and figure out ways to attract them.

There are purely objective questions, which take into account a potential customer's size, location, and landscape needs and, then, there are more subjective questions like rating how loyal a customer might be and what his/her/its values are.

Such criteria will allow you to more efficiently target the customers you want and develop a protocol to politely say "no" to the ones you don't.

Once you find and attract your desired clientele, it's time to start securing your contracts by building a strong relationship.

STEPPING STONE 2:
LEVELS OF CUSTOMER RELATIONSHIP

The first step to strengthening customer relations is to recognize where you stand with them.

We provide members with worksheets that have questions pertaining to their customers' experience and numeric goals for retention, referrals, requests, etc.

But, even if you don't have these worksheets, you can still take stock of your customer relations by listing the top paying 20% of your customers and ranking them on a one to five scale, with five being the best.

1. VENDOR

If your customer treats you like a "vendor", then they see you no differently than the latest dishwasher soap - to them, you're just a commodity. If your competitor can offer a better price, better experience, or has better referrals, then you'd better start packing. Additionally, if this is how your customers see you, you will have to bid jobs low just to keep them, and will soon find yourself working harder for less money.

2. TRUSTED ADVISOR

At this level, the customer respects your opinion. You know you've reached this level when you start to get calls with questions about the customer's landscape. Another sign is getting new jobs without having to bid on them. A respected opinion might not be enough to stop a customer from switching to a better-priced competitor, but at least they might give you a last look before deciding.

3. PARTNER

This is the level where things really start to shift. Your customer sees you as an equal, not just a service they pay for. This is when the customer won't make a move without consulting you or, if you mess up, you'll have leeway. This stage usually accounts for about 10-20% of customers.

4. RAVING FAN

This step is more proactive than a "partner" insofar as the customer will actually talk about you to people in his/her social circles. At this stage it would take something major to mess up the relationship. You might receive personalized cards on holidays or birthdays, and it would be a good idea to reciprocate this exchange. And, the best part? Referrals. This is where going that extra mile to satisfy your customer starts to pay off.

5. EVANGELIST

These are the customers that preach to friends, relatives, social circles, and on social media about how great you and your company are. When other potential customers see this level of enthusiasm, it's better than any amount of marketing money can buy. It's the real deal. Make sure to take care of these customers the best, as they are your most valuable resource when it comes to building your reputation and getting new business. An excitement level such as this usually occurs after customers can entrust you with critical jobs knowing that you will hit it out of the park every time. This is where you should aim to get all your customers - Evangelists.

> **ACTION STEP:** List your favorite customers and rank your relationship with them on a 1-5 scale (Vendor to Evangelist). Now, write down one thing you can do for each customer that will help push their ranking to the next level.

STEPPING STONE 3: BUILDING RELATIONSHIPS

In the beginning, most customers will treat you like any of their other *Vendors*. The key to transitioning from this first step to *Trusted Advisor* and beyond is to change their experience with you from one that is transactional to one that is relational.

If you've ever stayed at a Motel 6 vs staying at the Ritz, you know what I mean. At a Motel 6, it's purely transactional. You give them money, get your key, and that's it. At the Ritz, they greet you by name and will go the extra mile to take care of whatever you need, ensuring your experience is pleasurable. Sure, the level of accommodations are much nicer but, if employees at the Ritz started treating people like they do at Motel 6, you can bet their clients wouldn't be as quick to pay a premium price just for a nice room.

GET TO KNOW YOUR CUSTOMER

If you want to start fortifying customer relationships, start learning about customers on an additional level, other than a basic transactional one.

What are their hobbies? Do they have a family? What are some other landscapes like, which they admire?

Ask customers questions in a casual way while you're having conversations and create a customer profile so when you meet with them again you can offer a more personalized experience.

MANAGE EXPECTATIONS

Another way to build healthy customer relationships is to make sure you both have a clear understanding of each other's expectations.

This doesn't only include contractual items like timelines and costs, but should leave room for the unknown, like the eventuality of rain or other unforeseen delays.

Whenever the unexpected arises, communication is key. Know your customer's preferred method of communication – call, fax, email, text, in-person – and touch base to keep them up-to-date.

Even if everything is going smoothly, check in at least once a week so they know you are continuing to look out for their needs.

ANTICIPATE NEEDS

The better you get to know your customers and their expectations, the better you'll be able to anticipate their needs and take actions that will really start to improve how they feel about you.

ED:

 I was once awarded a contract for grounds maintenance at the General Electric Corporation's World Headquarters and, after talking with the facilities manager, learned the CEO, Jack Welch, was an avid golfer and loved green grass. A few months later I was able to get the manager to budget some money for the renovation of an area known as the "East Lawn". This is the lawn all the executives passed in the morning on their way into the office. When we knew the CEO would be away on business, we killed the existing grass, power-sliced new seed into the lawns and fertilized heavily. In a few weeks, the new seed took root and greened up. A few months later, as Mr. Welch drove by the newly seeded area, he noticed the beautiful bright green lawn in this area. He commented to the facilities manager about how great the area looked and, when he asked why it looked so good, the manager said it had just been renovated. Then, Mr. Welch said those magic words, "Why doesn't the rest of the place look that good!" Literally, the next day we were given a contract to renovate all 25 acres of the property. Yes!

Information is powerful. The more you learn about your customers, manage their expectations, and anticipate their needs, the stronger the relationships you will forge.

STEPPING STONE 4: CUSTOMER TOUCH POINTS

Putting yourself in the shoes of your customer will give you a better idea of what areas of your business to improve.

This involves being aware of every way the customer experiences your company, from phone calls, to emails, to in-person meetings, to navigating the website, or dealing with your employees, etc. - what we like to call "Touch Points".

All these Touch Points have either a positive or negative feel for your customer. An inclusive list of Touch Points can be found on the Harvest Way website. It's worthwhile to survey certain valued customers to find out if there's anything about the way they interact with your company that you can improve.

STEPPING STONE 5: YOUR PEOPLE

Perhaps the most impactful and most difficult Touch Point to manage is your people.

Convincing your people that good customer service is paramount to the company's success can be difficult, but it all starts with how well you've embedded the belief into your company culture and hiring process. (*See: PEOPLE, BUCKET #2*)

Internal discussions about customer service, company rules for engaging with customers, and incentives for great customer service are tried and true methods for improving this Touch Point.

Another method is to empower a few trusted managers in your company to have a degree of pre-authorized financial freedom when it comes to fixing problems. Your customers will not only be pleased the problem is solved, but impressed by its quick resolution.

STEPPING STONE 6: CONFLICT RESOLUTION

No matter how well you plan or how well you train your people, there will always be occasions when things go wrong. What separates the wheat from the chaff is how you deal with the problem.

LISTEN

The best thing you can do any time a customer is upset is to allow them to blow off steam and listen to their complaint. You'd be surprised how many times this response is sufficient enough to solve a problem.

The worst thing you can do is to interrupt someone. If you'd like to ask questions to help fix or clear the matter up, wait until they are finished.

Be sure to restate the person's problem and acknowledge that you have heard what they have said.

OWN IT

Whatever problem someone has - own it! Don't blame the managers, the company, the alignment of the stars - don't tell them you're going to report it to whomever, tell them how YOU will work to fix it.

FIX IT

It helps to suggest ways to resolve the problem or ask the customer for advice. Once you've agreed on a solution, put 100% effort into fixing the problem as fast and correctly as possible.

HUG

Not literally, of course, but metaphorically give your customer a hug for whatever transgressions he/she may have felt. Send a basket of flowers, tickets to a movie, dinner to his/her favorite restaurant - you get the idea, but whatever you do, do it and do it right away.

If you handle problems correctly your customers will be happy, you will gain their respect, and even improve upon your existing relationships.

STEPPING STONE 7: RENEWALS

The average commercial landscape contract lasts from one to three years. It's important customers are delighted with your service long before the contract renewal date approaches. But, even if they are, sometimes they may still be required to bid the job because of extraneous department policies or new managers.

If you've done your job at forging a strong relationship, the people in the right positions will do everything possible to keep you. Every change has a learning curve and sticking with someone they know and even like makes things easier.

Even so, there are times when the contracts come down to numbers - pure and simple. If you have the right connections you can find out if there are any new budgetary constraints. If you don't, it's best to err on the safe side and think of ways to save the manager money without detracting from the property.

We've worked in the industry long enough to know that many residential contractors don't have contracts with their customers. This is an issue we strongly advise our clients to reconsider: Get contracts or written agreements with all your customers.

If you ever plan to sell your company, contracts and written agreements are tangible assets. In some states there exist clauses that do not allow certain types of contracts, so it's best to check regulations or have a lawyer read over the contracts before presenting them.

As your relationship with your customers continues to grow never take your relationship for granted and always ask yourself what you can be doing to make it better.

CUSTOMER EXERCISES

The Harvesters often refer to The Big 4. These are what we consider to be the absolute foundation pieces for an organization to be a success. We talked a little about the PEOPLE part and how it is the CENTRAL FOUNDATION piece.

Now, we are in the bucket of another one of the BIG 4 that we all must truly have mastery over.

All organizations must be able to -

"Find, Attract, Get On Board, Keep, and Grow the RIGHT Customers."
- The Harvesters

Also keep in mind -

"The Customer is ALWAYS Right, but you just might not have the Right Customer!" - The Harvesters

So, with this in mind, here are some items you should have in place:

Action Steps:

- Get out your customer list and review and rank all of your existing customers using an A-B-C scale.
- Who are your top 10 customers? Who is their primary contact person in your organization? When was the last time you spent some quality time with them?
- What is their current level of satisfaction? What needs to be done to remain at a high level?
- What is your game plan to renew this agreement?
- Which ones do you want to keep and grow? Which ones would you rather have do business with your competitor?
- Build a game plan for each level of customer to either keep and grow them or lose them in a positive professional manner.
- Have an alarm system in place that sounds the alarm when there is a customer change!

- Build a Job in Jeopardy and Lost Job Autopsy process in your organization: See more about these processes in The Harvest Way Academy, in our Customers Count area.

Note: These two processes are considered "best practices" that all organizations should know and practice. As you can probably tell, one process is a proactive process, while the other is more of what we call a "learning experience" or post mortem lesson learned.

Remember this -
"It's hard to make money on a job you don't have."
- Head Harvester Bill

Suggested Reading: *Raving Fans* by Ken Blanchard

BUCKET #4:
LEADERSHIP

Ask five people what it means to be a leader and you'll get five different answers. This is because not everyone leads the same way and the journey to becoming a strong leader is as much an inward one as it is an outward one.

While definitions on what this role entails may vary, the general sentiments remain similar: a leader is someone who knows how to identify and achieve goals and can inspire people to achieve them.

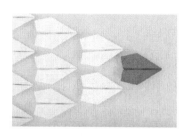

Having a clear vision, getting people to believe they are working towards something larger than themselves, and knowing your team's strengths and weaknesses (including your own!) are all building blocks of what it takes to be a great leader.

Whether you want this role or not, as the owner of your company, people are going to look to you for leadership - so you'd better be ready to step up and take command.

STEPPING STONE 1: LEADER ASSESSMENT

At its core, the definition of a strong leader is someone who inspires others to a goal that would otherwise be beyond what they could achieve.

Fortunately for you, if you're looking to pinpoint your strengths, weaknesses, and any other attributes as a leader, there are dozens of books, online resources, and tests available that will help you find and improve the areas you need to focus on.

In our Harvest Way Leadership guidebook, we encourage readers to really think about, even meditate on, what they believe makes an effective leader. Once this is clear in your mind you can list the

51

characteristics that contribute to each of these traits to put them into practice.

For example, an effective leader is more than someone who "makes decisions", but someone whose decisions keep others working toward a larger dream.

Assess your strengths and weaknesses as a leader so you can round out any deficiencies.

STEPPING STONE 2: INSPIRE A VISION

If you don't know where you're going, how will you know when you get there?

The answer is, you won't.

Unless you have a vision - a clear idea of where you want to take your company and what you want it to achieve - you will be a slave to chance circumstances.

Step back from the day-to-day rat race and write your vision. Creating a detailed plan on how to achieve this vision will be worth your while financially and spiritually. It will elevate what you're doing from "work" to "building something great" with the sum of all your labors.

Your core values and virtues will help provide direction for your vision.

As the leader, it's your job to make your expectations clear to all the people who are working for you. Your vision should be concise and understood by everyone in your company. Want to become the industry expert in tree trimming? Write that vision on the walls and then, whenever you are faced with a decision, ask yourself which choice will best accomplish that goal.

The intent is to lead people to victory, not push or pull. Encourage, engage, involve, and challenge.

When people know where they are headed, have faith in your ability to lead them, and are part of the process, you'll see your vision take on a group momentum and have a life of its own.

STEPPING STONE 3:
MODEL THE WAY - SUCCESS BEHAVIORS

As the head honcho, your day-to-day actions will resonate throughout your company and set the tone for how others behave. If you communicate by yelling and insulting, it's unlikely others will be patient with each other nor work well as a team. Likewise, if you display traits you believe in, i.e. honesty, patience, etc., you will create a work environment that naturally caters to the values you've demonstrated.

The behaviors that build a healthy work environment are what we call "Success Behaviors". These behaviors, which start with you, can be incorporated into the company's core values and can be further actualized by writing them down.

For instance, let's say one of your core values is "hard work". If your employees see you coming in late and leaving early every day with a golf bag slung over your shoulder, you're going to have a tough time getting people to fall in line with this value. To be blunt, they'll see you as a bullshitter. Without actions to back up your words and company vision, your words will carry little weight - or, as we like to say, "taste your words before feeding them to others".

After years spent working and consulting in the landscape industry, we've found there are certain Success Behaviors that create a healthy company.

Things like listening, being prepared, being on time, and engaging others are some of the basic beneficial ones, while whining, fussing, criticizing, and complaining are harmful.

So, take a good look at yourself. Are you a model of what you expect from others?

If you'd like to get a more detailed understanding of how to generate and practice behaviors that will improve your company culture and support your company vision, check out our Harvest Way Academy Leadership handbooks and videos.

> **ACTION STEP:** Write a list of your company's core values and brainstorm the beneficial Success Behaviors you can demonstrate as a leader to reinforce these.

STEPPING STONE 4: SHARPEN THE SKILLS

While self-improvement is a lifelong pursuit, we've identified four fundamental skills to focus on if you want to increase the success of your company.

MENTOR

Have a mentor and be a mentor. You're trying to get the greatest potential out of yourself and others. The best way to do this is learn from those who are better than you and learn how to inspire those who don't know as much. If you don't already have a mentor, you can find one by reading, going to seminars, or using resources like the NALP Adopt a Mentor Trailblazer Program. Sometimes, just learning the thought processes of another person who inspires you is enough. If you're looking for a more personal interaction, then don't approach a potential mentor asking for some of his/her time, but instead ask yourself what you can do that will help improve his/her quality of life. It can be humbling to admit a lack of knowledge and learn from a teacher, but that humility is a valuable lesson, too. It's impossible to be a good teacher if you were never a student.

When it comes to mentoring, find a student who has the potential to be groomed into a leadership role that will benefit you and your company. Your role is not to boss that person around, but set challenges, offer advice, and provide guidance.

DELEGATION

We see it all the time, people trying to be administrator, supervisor, foreman, planter, trimmer - but when it comes to running a business, it's not a one man show. You can't do it all yourself. Learn what areas you can delegate to others and then learn to let go. We know the process can be scary, especially as certain roles carry more weight than others. The key is to create a system where you teach others to take on more responsibility, assignments, and authority and earn your trust. You need to provide people with enough direction on how to do their job and then get the hell out of the way. Inability to delegate results in limited company growth and unnecessary pressure on the owner. If you want to learn more on how to strategically hire and train people in the landscape industry to take over company responsibilities, you can check out our Harvest Way Academy section on Leadership. As the leader of a company, your job should be working on the business, not in it.

ORGANIZATION

STOP. Take a picture of your desk right now. Does it look organized? This is a regular exercise we do with our clients to see how organized they really are. And, it doesn't stop with your physical office. Look at your computer. Is client info, financial info, sales data, etc., easily accessible? Can you easily figure out where each of your crews are today? Are your tools and workspaces orderly? If you're spending more time looking for an item or information than using it, you're wasting your time. Even though it may seem like a herculean task getting organized, the amount of time you'll save in the long run will make it worth your efforts.

TIME MANAGEMENT

The first step in managing your time is figuring out where it all goes. Make a chart and figure out the areas where you spend most of your time. Now ask yourself in which area you get the highest return. Which area brings you the most stress? According to the Franklin Covey Method discussed in the book "*7 Habits of Highly Effective People*", the most successful businessmen in the world are experts at time management. A time management exercise you can put into practice is to get out your calendar and see how much time you have booked for the next two weeks. If there's a ton of open space and you're not blocking off time for things like getting organized, then you'll find trivial tasks will easily sneak in and steal your hours. Check out our Academy for more time management tips and techniques.

STEPPING STONE 5: BE A LEARNER

A business is like a shark - if it isn't always adapting, changing, innovating . . . moving, it'll die. As the leader of a business, it's your job to always be learning and coming up with new ways to move your business forward. Having a solid core belief of why you're in business, along with a clear vision of where you want to go, will help inspire your goals, which will dictate your learning material. To always be in an environment of personal, mental, and spiritual growth, surround yourself with others who are on the never-ending path of self-improvement. Read, watch videos, listen to books on tape, attend conferences, classes, and events. Figure out which growth methods stimulate you best and dive in head first.

STEPPING STONE 6:
TEAM BUILDING AND MOTIVATION

Harvester Bill says, "Great leaders inspire individuals to become part of a team that can accomplish exponentially more than one person ever could". This skill involves coaching individuals to unlock the potential of their skill and claim a position of value within an organization. It also involves knowledge of group dynamics and how to resolve conflicts before they tear a group apart.

Most struggling companies we work with practice conflict avoidance instead of resolution, knowingly ignoring problems and hoping they'll go away. Eventually, this tactic will fail and the results can be catastrophic. We suggest tackling conflicts as soon as they arise. Divorce your emotions from a conflict, identify its root cause, take measures to resolve it, and be grateful for the learning opportunity.

If the problem is external to your business, then determine if you need to seek legal counsel or if you can cut out that element from your path to success.

If it's internal, then set aside time, sit down with the opposing parties, and allow all sides to voice their feelings and opinions before coming to a decision.

The best course of action is to identify and choose team members from the start who will work well together and give teams assignments that will set common goals and help build bonds.

When picking team leaders, do so wisely, always keeping an eye out for a possible successor to other roles, even your own. Determine which skills these potential successors need to grow so you can sharpen them and devote time to helping them develop. This will create an environment of gratitude, companionship, and, ultimately, growth - which is, after all, the aim of your business.

LEADER'S EXERCISE

When Ed and I visit organizations either during our Harvest Assessments, "Tune Ups", or with our 1 to 1 Coaching program, we learn and see right away why some organizations do so well and why others seem not be to "harvesting their potential" that well. I guess those of you reading this right now are getting a little nervous . . . and, for good reason. The fact of the matter is that it ALL STARTS and STOPS with YOU, the Leader! We have found that with virtually every organization that the "limits to success" of an organization sit right with the leader.

So, with this in mind, here are some action steps and questions for you leaders.

- Have a 360 Review performed on you, the leader.

This is a significant and intense review process that gives the leader feedback from several angles / vantage points, or a 360 view, from the people they interact with and lead, including their peers, their subordinates, and other levels in the organization.

Note: The 360 Review should be performed by the HR department or an outside HR experienced professional.

- After the 360 Review, decide on what one skill and one behavior, if really tuned up, would have the most positive impact on you and how you lead.
- Put a plan in place to build or sharpen the one skill and one behavior and write it down!

- Consider joining a PEER Group: See and learn more about this with the Harvest Leaders' Group program.
- Seek and take good counsel: Hire a Coach / Mentor if you haven't already done so.
- Ask your people what they think you should start doing or do more of.
- Next, ask them what you should do less of or just stop doing.
- And, finally, ask them this: Congratulations! You now own the company! What are the first three things you are going to do?

One great current spiritual leader that I listen to and read from is Rick Warren, Head Pastor at Saddleback Church in Lake Forest, California, and author of The Purpose Driven Life. During one of his messages, he taught us that there are basically three key qualities to learn to become a good leader and they are: Integrity – Humility – Generosity.

Integrity: Including sound ethics, trustworthiness, being truthful, and having strong moral principles.

Humility: A modest view of one's own importance, humbleness: derived from the word humus, meaning of the earth, and humor, not taking yourself so seriously.

Generosity: Not so much with money, but with one's time. There are few things worth more than time. It is spent and never retrieved. So, where are you spending your time? Often, just your positive presence is a powerful use of your time.

Which of these three qualities do you embody? Which ones need some work?

BUCKET #5:
BUSINESS

If your business is the vehicle you're driving toward success, then these are the gears that make it run. This bucket covers all the foundations, systems, and strategies you should make sure are tuned up and in excellent working order.

We know that for guys like us, who like to work with our hands, some of the business essentials, such as cost tracking, budgeting, legal documents, and banking, can be boring and are only all too easy to procrastinate. But, if your goal is to work smarter, not harder, and grow your business into a stable and profitable entity, then making sure you dot and cross these Business Bucket i's and t's could be the difference between your failure or success.

Consulting this chapter now and making sure you have these key systems running smoothly will ensure you're not reacting to problems down the road that could have been easily avoided.

STEPPING STONE 1: FOUNDATIONS

Before you start growing your business, you'll want to make sure the foundation it's rooted in is solid. Here are a few key areas to focus on:

HIRE A CPA

Having accurate bookkeeping and financing will ensure bills are paid on time and give you a realistic perspective about your company's health. Interview several accountants and find one you like. Even if it seems out of your range, a good accountant pays long-term dividends and will help you get your business off to a strong start. A good accountant doesn't just help you with taxes.

He should help you understand your business and support you in building profits by cutting expenses, reducing your taxes, and pricing your work correctly.

LIABILITY AND INSURANCE

There are liabilities you can avoid and ones you can't. The most costly are those that are avoidable, but for which you have no insurance coverage. The three biggest incidents that fall into this category are environmental, safety, and personnel claims. There are niche professionals who will review your policies for a fee and excel in finding chinks in your insurance armor. If you can't afford these experts, be proactive and make a list of all the areas in which you feel you might be liable. Call the fire department and even city council to find out information. Once this list is complete call your insurance company to negotiate fees and make sure you're covered for the situations you've researched.

BANKS

Don't keep all your eggs in one basket and only work with one bank. Mergers happen and, if a bank goes out of business or calls in a loan, it's good to have your bases covered with another. We like to suggest a large bank and a local one. When dealing with banks, it's best to think of them for what they are: a business run by business people. Bankers try to negotiate the highest interest rates they can get. If they know you, trust you, and become your friend, they're likely to be reasonable and get you a loan at a competitive rate. When it comes to business, money is like oxygen - if your business doesn't have enough, it suffocates. Establish good relationships and lines of credit with banks so, if your business lacks for air, it has a reliable respirator it can use.

LEGAL STRUCTURE

There are five basic legal structures for a business in the USA: Sole Proprietorship, LLC, S-Corp, C-Corp, and General Partnership. In order to create the largest cash value in your company, you need to know the right entity. Online searches are cheap, but usually produce cookie cutter results that are not always best. Attorneys and accountants are more expensive, but stay in business because they produce results. When looking for the structure that's right for you, consider how you want to protect assets, flexibility with regard to owner's perks, tax advantages, equity creation, and, the best option if or when you ever decide to sell your business. These elements will help give you direction for making the right choice. For numerous reasons our preference is the Sub-S Corporation, though we urge you to come to your own conclusion after seeking professional advice.

WEB PRESENCE

Conduct online research on your company's name and services before pulling the trigger on branding it. If you have a company name you like, make sure an appropriate web address (URL) is available to go with it. If it is, lock down all the possible domain iterations.

We once worked with a client who only purchased the domain for the abbreviated name of his company because he thought it sounded better. His competitor ended up purchasing the domain with the full name of his company, redirecting traffic to his website. It cost the client a lot of money in legal fees and hard merchandising, not to mention all the headache of explaining to his customers why the company changed its name.

STEPPING STONE 2: BASIC BUSINESS SYSTEMS

Once you have the foundations covered, it's time to organize a few key systems that you will need to have in place as your business grows. Not having these in order would be like trimming a lawn with a pair of scissors - you might get the job done, but it will be a huge headache.

PRICING

New business owners are often afraid to charge what the job costs to stay afloat. As a result, more than half of the landscape companies in the U.S. are out of business within 10 years because they don't earn a profit. Breakdown your costs and make sure markups for labor and materials generate enough profit to keep your business healthy. There are four basic ways to markup prices: materials, direct costs, labor and burden, and labor and materials.

Each of these has benefits and drawbacks. To learn more, visit our classes online or research books dedicated to landscape industry pricing.

BILLING

Having a system in place so you bill in an accurate and timely manner is important to keeping your finances on track. Have an automated process that sends bills to customers in increments of time (i.e. 15 days, 30 days, etc.). Keep an eye on your Accounts Receivables, which is the outstanding money that is owed from your customers to your company. If these are funds you are counting on, but don't have yet, that means you are the one taking out loans or risks on money you're owed! We like to suggest negotiating "up front" payments with new customers so you're always working with their money and not yours. Consider invoicing at the beginning of the month and not the end, which is when you should save invoices for any additional work.

ACCOUNTS RECEIVABLES

Lack of cash is the single biggest reason companies go bankrupt. So, we say, "COLLECT THE MONEY!" It's your money and, if customers are not paying on time or are trying to take advantage of the terms, it's time to start buckling down. Make sure your contracts are crystal clear so there is no misunderstanding on payment dates. Secondly, start calling customers as soon as the terms exceed that of the contract. Don't wait for it to go on for 90 days and have to threaten to stop services.

COST TRACKING

Forming a reliable system to monitor your Profit and Loss statements (P&Ls) will give you a plan on where to take your business and how to improve it. The best way to do this is by tracking the direct costs on jobs as they are performed until completion, and then comparing the actual numbers to the budget estimate. If the hours or costs are high, figure out why so you can better create future estimates and bids. This can be done manually or on a computer. Even if you run smaller maintenance jobs, you can cost track the jobs collectively instead of by each individual employee. Cost tracking provides a huge opportunity to generate higher profits and it's one of our favorite topics to elucidate upon in our Harvest Way Academy.

CONTRACTS AND AGREEMENTS

You will keep more of your money if you have clear contracts in place. In the event of disagreements, it will give you leverage to bargain for what you're owed. Even if you're only doing residential work and think that verbal agreements are all you need, you're wrong. If you ever want to sell your company, it will be difficult to prove it has any value without real contracts. We also suggest signed non-compete contracts with your employees and subcontractors and to use your own contracts whenever possible. If someone insists on using theirs, send it to an attorney and redline any stipulations that might prove detrimental to your right to get paid.

FINANCIAL SOFTWARE

Though there are plenty of software programs out there, the most popular in our industry is QuickBooks, which accounts for around 95% of users.

STEPPING STONE 3: PLANNING

A vision not written down is only a dream. A plan is what a vision becomes when it's in writing.

A plan determines the steps needed to execute your vision. Without a plan, your life is just getting through a series of today's.

How sad when an owner finally sits down to calculate the company's net worth only to realize that years of hard work resulted in little to no equity because there was no plan in place.

Most owners, ourselves included, usually have to get to a place where planning is an absolute necessity before we invest the time and effort needed to write one.

The power of a written business plan is that it connects all aspects of your business in a logical way that makes it easier to make day-to-day decisions that lead you toward your ultimate goal.

A good rule is to set aside 1% of your working time throughout the year to plan for the 99% of time you'll be working.

Review your accomplishments, identify your current situation, and prepare your future vision. Create a SWOT analysis of your Strengths, Weaknesses, Opportunities, and Threats (SWOT).

Refer to your plan at least once a quarter to make sure you're on course. Review your accomplishments, identify your current situation, and prepare your benchmark measurements (i.e. budget goals, additional sales, etc.) with detailed action steps on how to get there.

> **ACTION STEP:** Business planning is habit forming, so get your calendar out <u>right now</u> and set aside a date you will begin to plan.

STEPPING STONE 4: BUDGET

When it comes to succeeding in the landscape industry, think of a "Budget" as your game plan and a "Profit and Loss Statement" as your game review.

A budget is a projection of what you think you're going to do in sales and costs. This projection helps reduce unknown gambles you might take with your operations because you can begin to measure financial performance on a monthly basis.

Most companies base their budget on what happened the previous year. A very basic way to do this is to take your sales numbers and estimate where you think they're going to be for the coming year. Keep monthly tabs on your projected gross margins versus the real numbers and adjust your sales and labor strategies accordingly.

Remember, a gross margin is what's left after all your expenses are accounted for. If this number is too low, you will not be able to pay your overheads or make a fair profit.

We recommend bringing on a professional to help you create a budget, or visiting the Harvest Way Academy to learn more about budgets that are specific for the landscape industry. Trends such as only making 6-12% profit on jobs and spending 25-55% of your revenue on labor costs are the norm for our industry. Working examples of mini-budgets that track the costs for construction, maintenance, and sales departments can be found at the Harvest Way Academy. These will help you gain a better understanding of how to organize and build budgets on your own.

Because margins in our industry are usually so tight, learning how to correctly budget will mean the success or failure of your company.

STEPPING STONE 5:
PROFIT & LOSS STATEMENTS (P&Ls)

This is the method companies use to measure how its finances are doing each month - think of it as a way of keeping score. With this tool you don't need to wait until the end of the year to figure out how you've been doing, but can immediately react to any problem or negative trend that might be developing.

P&Ls are monthly and annual statements that provide a summary of revenues, direct costs (aka Cost of Goods or COG), indirect costs, and General and Administrative Expenses (G&A).

Most companies dismiss P&Ls as a tool their accountants use for tax purposes. However, when setup correctly, it can help with job estimates, pricing, and measuring performance.

Think about it: When you know how much "cash" it costs to do a job, you can measure how good your estimate was, if you over- or under-stocked materials, and if the crews performed efficiently within the budgeted hours.

The gross margin left after every job is a simple way to determine how profitable it was and where there's room for improvement. It is therefore crucial to obtain the gross margins for every profit center the company is involved with - landscape maintenance, landscape construction, etc.

To start performing monthly P&L reviews, you can visit our Harvest Way Academy for worksheets and courses or hire an outside accounting firm. If you opt for the latter, agree upon a monthly date for the firm to generate reports so you can stay on top of the numbers. We usually like to suggest seeing a report for the previous month on the 15th of each current month. Be sure all your statements include percentages next to the numbers so you can get a better idea of its growth or shrinkage.

You can compare how your company is doing with others of a similar size by purchasing an Operating and Cost Study from the National Association of Landscape Professionals (NALP). A simple report that costs less than $50 can show you valuable information such as where you might be paying too much for things like insurance or maintenance. This report might save you thousands of dollars.

If you are not doing monthly P&L reviews, it is absolutely imperative to start so you know what the score is as you play the game of landscaping.

STEPPING STONE 6: JOB COST TRACKING

In the landscape industry the best way to measure the profitability of your business is to track the costs of each job. While there are many small costs that add up, it's easiest to start by monitoring the largest cost: labor.

You can do this by accounting for the direct cost on jobs as crews perform them and then comparing the actual data to the budget estimate.

Keeping an eye on man-hours and productivity will determine if the job is going to be over or under budget. Simply take the estimated hours you've allotted for a job and start subtracting hours as the payroll comes in to see if you're going to be over or under the mark. If the hours are going to be over budget, you have the opportunity to take immediate action to correct the problem.

Setting up an effective job cost tracking system is one of the first things we do when we come in to help a new client. It's low hanging fruit with high rewards, and is a necessary system to have in place if you want to grow and be profitable.

> **ACTION STEP:** Even if you don't have large jobs and only have small jobs, cost tracking is still a necessity. You can track jobs collectively by the crew, by the week, day, or hour - find something that works and then pick your easiest job to track and start now!

STEPPING STONE 7: EXIT STRATEGY

When you sow a field full of wheat, the end goal isn't to just grow a bunch of crops, but to harvest them for food and profit.

Same, too, with your business. After all the hard labor you've put into growing and maintaining your business, you should always keep in mind its final harvest - the time when you plan to sell.

As business consultants in the landscape industry, this is something we put into each client's head from the get-go. It will help you increase the value of your company, and leave things so you're not scrambling last minute when you're ready to step back and retire. It will keep you from reacting last minute to any unforeseen life events that might occur and allow you to sell near the top of the business cycle so you can get what you deserve: the highest dollar value for all your years of sweat and hard work.

Even if you're one of those work-until-the-day-I-die-ers, remember that every business will eventually change hands, whether it's during your lifetime or after. If you want to come out of this landscaping game on top, then it is best to heed the advice of the famous military strategist Sun Tzu:

> *"Victorious warriors win first and then go to war, while defeated warriors go to war first and then seek to win."*

THE 3 ALIGNING FACTORS FOR SELLING

1. Are you financially ready and prepared to sell?

Sure, determining your objectives and goals takes soul searching, but it also boils down to answering a list of practical questions: How long do you want to remain active in the business? How much money will it take for you to be financially stable after you exit? Do you want to completely cash out, receive a portion of the purchase price over time, partially exit, transfer the business to an employee, family member, stranger . . . well, you get the idea. There's a ton to go over here which is why we've dedicated two Harvest Way ebooks and over a dozen videos to this topic in our Academy.

2. What is the current value and marketability of your business?

This requires first understanding and being able to identify the two types of buyers who are going to be interested in your business:

- Strategic Buyer: These buyers want to add a revenue synergy to an existing business. Once this buyer purchases your company, the total costs of running it will decrease while administrative, advertising, or other duplications are downsized. These sorts of buyers place value on the synergy your company will offer theirs.

- Financial Buyer: These types of buyers are looking for a stand-alone business that has a healthy ROI (return on investment) and cash flow. They usually won't make significant changes to your company if it's set up well and they tend to place value on stability and how easy the business is to maintain.

After identifying which buyer you'd like to attract, you can determine the value of your business by looking at things like its Asset Value, Comparable Transaction Value, Income Capitalization, and Discounted Cash Flow, or variations of these categories. While this might seem like a lot to chew on, you can think of it as a standardized way to show the cash flow the buyer can expect to generate after acquisition.

The easiest and most trusted way to do this is to get a verified business valuation or market assessment of your business by an appraiser, CPA, or business broker. You can make sure you're ready to be assessed before the broker comes by downloading the Harvest Way Green Exit from our Academy. The document includes a detailed list of the elements that will increase or decrease the value of a green business.

3. Are the market conditions right for a sale?

It should come as no surprise that market conditions are cyclical and subject to more changes than seasons in the year. Good news is, while things around you might be out of your control, the health of your business isn't.

Keeping records and building a predictable and sustained cash flow will enhance the perceived value of your business. The longer you have records, the more stable it will appear.

Things like your business's growth rate, pricing history, structure, and customer retention rate will be of interest to a person looking to buy.

As you move closer toward selling your business, keep Gross Margins as high as possible to fetch a better price. If you've had several impressive profitable years in a row, it might be worth selling early so you can get the maximum rewards for your labor. If the years haven't been so good and you foresee a turnaround, consider sticking things out for a while longer while your company's value bounces back.

Either way, you'll want to make sure that when you're selling your business there is a good market and you are both financially and emotionally ready for the move.

> **ACTION STEP:** Make a checklist to determine if you're ready to sell and be sure to include detailed action steps you can take to increase the value of your company. If this seems like too much work, you can always check out the Harvest Way Green Exit-1 book at the Harvest Way Academy.

VALUE DRIVERS FOR THREE LANDSCAPE INDUSTRIES

1. DESIGN BUILD

These types of landscape companies have very little recurring revenue, making their valuations lower than other industries in the field. As a result, the business's reputation and a proven ability for its sales team to generate new business will attract more buyers and a better price. We encourage design build companies to diversify their services and offer things like irrigation, hardscapes, swimming pools, or whatever else might complement its core business model. Another approach is to get creative with financing models for the buyer. If a buyer is able to finance a higher purchase price, this will result in you getting more money for your business.

2. LANDSCAPE MAINTENANCE

The value for this type of business fluctuates between extreme highs and lows depending on the market. The best selling plan for a Landscape Maintenance company is to prepare the business for sale well in advance of a planned exit and make a move when the market is right. To maximize the value of this type of business, the owner will want to maintain a diverse customer base, have a record of maintaining long term customer contracts, have attractive facilities and equipment, and a solid history of customers who pay their bills on time.

3. TREE CARE COMPANY

This type of business has recurring revenue streams, non-recurring components, and project components. The value of such a business is based on its established brand name, its licenses, certifications, and insurance, the quality of its employees, and records proving the financial success of its pricing strategies.

EXIT STAGE LEFT

Writing a detailed plan is key to a successful exit. You'll want to make sure to revisit and update the document as needed if there are any personal, financial, or industry changes that take place. It's also a wise decision to have a group of advisors - professionals, like an exit-planning specialist - look over your final plans. Another option is to check out our Harvest Way Green Exit for detailed checklists, specialists, and information on how to plan your exit.

BUSINESS EXERCISES

We have covered a LOT of area in this bucket so let's work on some of the key takeaways we have covered.

Ask yourself some of these questions or get these key business pieces in play:

Planning

- Do you have a plan? Is it in writing? Do all of your key people have a copy?
- Do you have buy in with the plan?
- When was the last time, if ever, that you have created a plan?
- What are the top five goals your organization wants to accomplish next year? How will these be measured?
- What are the top five goals to be accomplished in the next three years? How will these be measured?

Remember what the Harvesters have to say about planning:

"No Plan – No Way!"
The Harvesters

It will be very hard to accomplish your goals if there is no plan to measure and assess your goal achievement. So, learn how to put a plan together. The Harvest Way Academy has a whole section on planning and you should plan on going through this great lesson.

Business Basics

- Review your process of estimating and pricing your work. Where can this be improved?

   Action Step: Review each construction job once completed for its profitability. Review your maintenance jobs monthly to see if they are tracking well on their budgeted Gross Margin. Make needed adjustments to your estimating and pricing processes. You do have a process right?

- o Are you making a fair profit, say 10-15% net? If yes, then proceed to the next section of this book. If not or if you don't know, yikes!

Action Step: Build and use a Profit and Loss Statement and keep it current.

- o What is your current Gross Margin overall? By revenue streams? Note: You will need to track Gross Margin very carefully and regularly - weekly for construction and monthly for maintenance.

Action Step: Build a mini budget process. This tracks your revenue and gross margin in real time. Probably one of the most important financial tools that can help you make money or at least identify what areas need help is the Harvesters "Mini Budget". Check it out in the Harvest Academy.

- o Accounts Receivable: How much money is owed to you that is over 60 days past your invoice date? The answer should be 0! Build an Accounts Receivable Process and TRACK IT like you MEAN IT! You can perform PERFECTLY in every aspect of business BUT, if you don't collect your money owed in a timely manner, ALL IS FOR NAUGHT!

Remember -

Your customers will expect many things from you. You, on the other hand, only expect one thing from your customer: PAYMENT ON TIME!

BUCKET #6:
OPERATIONS

They say that God is in the details - that attention to the smaller things reaps big rewards. Well, the daily Operations of your company are those details.

These are the systems you need in place so jobs will run smoothly even if you're not there. These are the systems that handle all the "stuff that happens" when they happen.

When operations are done well, an observer will hardly notice they're taking place; however, when they're done poorly, your company will appear unprofessional and disorganized.

About a year ago, we received one of those calls from a client that makes you need to sit down: one of his men was killed on the job. He was blowing freshly cut grass off the sidewalk near a mall. His back was toward traffic.

When he stepped backwards on the street to get a better angle, he was clipped by a car taking a right-hand turn, dying on impact. Earlier that day, our client had held and documented his company's daily safety meeting, which, ironically, happened to be on "being aware of your surroundings". Had this meeting never taken place and not been signed by each of the employees in attendance, it's doubtful whether our client would still have his company.

What makes the Operations Bucket so powerful is that it includes tangible steps you can immediately put in place to save you time, money, and even the future of your company.

STEPPING STONE 1: SAFETY

Accidents happen. And, while you can't control the unpredictable whims of fate, you can prepare for them with a comprehensive safety program.

ACCIDENT PREVENTION

Safety starts with the owner and has a trickle-down effect. If employees see the owner pick up a leaf blower without earmuffs or enter a hazardous area without a safety hat, you'd better believe they'll begin to mimic that casual safety attitude.

However, there are tried and true steps you can take to build safety into your culture, avoiding expensive fines, cutting down on the occurrences of onsite accidents, protecting your employees, saving money on worker's compensation and insurance costs, and avoiding a bankrupting lawsuit.

Being prudent in your hiring process and making it a rule not to hire anyone who seems reckless is a good place to start. Once a new person is on board have them complete a mandatory new hire safety program.

For ideas of what this program should look like, check out the Harvest Way Academy online Safety Program.

Additional safety programs can be found online with the NALP, the National Association of Landscape Professionals.

Other preventative measures include daily tailgate safety meetings before starting on a job site and requiring training and certifications for the operation of any dangerous equipment or jobs. This includes, but is not limited to, things like: driving company vehicles, operating powerful machinery, pruning trees, handling dangerous chemicals, and lifting heavy loads.

We know this may seem a bit much but, with the average cost of a back injury anywhere between $60-100k, it's worth it to make sure you cut down on as many incidents as possible and cover yourself with evidence of existing programs.

Hire an outside insurance/injury expert to make sure your company is in compliance with county and state safety standards. Insurance MOD rates are determined by the number and dollar value of worker's compensation claims filed against your company. If there are a few accidents during a particular year, you will end up paying a higher insurance premium in the following years. Likewise, if there are no accidents, the rate will decrease. Accidents landing an employee in the hospital for more that 24 hours will get you an expensive visit from OSHA, in addition to a whole bunch of other agency fines.

ACCIDENT RESPONSE

An important element of any well-rounded safety program is being prepared for accidents when they occur.

A good Accident Response program entails having the necessary equipment ready in case there's an on-site illness, injury, or chemical spill.

Provide Personal Protection Equipment (PPEs) for all your employees.

Goggles, ear protectors, gloves, and proper shoes should be the standard. Things like first aid kits, extra water, eye wash kits, and spill kits are also a good idea.

We even advise people to have a back up PR program in place in case things really hit the fan.

A strong safety program is usually the area in which our clients are most vulnerable so, before you start optimizing all your other operations, build a strong safety foundation.

ACCIDENT REVIEW

After an accident happens, investigate its cause and learn how to root it out so it doesn't happen again.

Create Accident Report Sheets for employees at the scene of the accident to fill out. Read these carefully as they might just save you and your crew from having to deal with hN the same mistake twice.

STEPPING STONE 2: STRUCTURE/CREW SET UP

We call it the "morning circus".

Employees show up to work in the morning not knowing which project they're assigned to or what equipment and material they need.

We've seen up to 30 men scurry around for over an hour just trying to get organized. At one company we visited, we calculated the wasted time resulting from a lack of organization cost the owners more than $110,000 a year.

It pays to schedule, plan, and have dependable chiefs who can manage their crews when you can't be at the job site. We know this can be like pulling teeth for most contractors, so we've included a few of the helpful strategies we give our Harvest Way members to get your momentum rolling:

TIP ONE: GET A WHITEBOARD

The size and numbers of boards are dependent on the size of your staff.

Use black electrical tape to divide the board(s) into a grid, where you can write the names of workers down the column on the left and days of the week(s) across the top row.

Fill this grid with information for where each worker is supposed to be, what team they're on, and details about the job they're supposed to execute.

Make index cards that represent trucks and limited equipment and use Velcro or magnets to stick these up and assign them to workers throughout the week.

You can even put envelopes next to each employee's name in which you can give notes or messages about the specific job on which they're working.

TIP TWO: TEACH YOUR CHIEFS

You can't be everywhere at once and you don't have the time to communicate the same message over and over again to all your employees about the ever-changing details of a job site.

Make sure you have the right amount of leaders to workers on a job site. Too many of either will prove cumbersome and inefficient. We call it the "Chief to Indian ratio".

Having a small circle of site-specific chiefs that you can touch base with every day and update and educate will free you from needing to be in every place at once.

If you need more "Chiefs", promote the strongest worker with the best leadership skills.

TIP THREE: PREPARE THE NIGHT BEFORE

Don't leave a mess for the morning. Take care of things like fixing damaged equipment, fueling trucks, putting away keys, and writing the next morning's job sequence the day before.

Tidy up after workers finish at the job site for the day. If needed, hire an extra hand or two. Paying one person to work a few prep hours at night makes much more financial sense than paying 30 people to waste one hour in the morning.

STEPPING STONE 3: EQUIPMENT PURCHASING

STICK TO A BRAND

When it comes to using equipment and machinery such as mowers, blowers, and trucks, find a brand you like and stick to it.

This is a best practice of nearly all the larger landscape companies.

The reasons for doing this are plenty:

- It's easier to stock parts when you're buying the same brand.
- Repair mechanics can become familiar with a brand, making them better at preventative care and maintenance, while establishing relationships with its support crew.
- Crews are more proficient in operating the equipment, resulting in fewer accidents.
- The more you purchase from a brand, dealers will become more loyal to you and give you better prices.

When buying equipment, make sure it's something your inventory needs, and not just an impulse buy because of a good price or based on a feeling.

Walk through your shop and conduct an equipment utilization rate. Refer to this rate whenever making purchasing decisions.

Other factors to influence your decision should be based on research regarding the reliability, ease, and cost of equipment maintenance.

PROPER USAGE

The lifespan of your equipment depends on how well it's treated.

Even if you try to communicate to your employees how expensive the equipment is, the cost may not translate since they did not foot the bill. Rather than hoping people will take care of the equipment, build an equipment incentive program.

Make an equipment list and hold one person on each crew responsible for ensuring the items are returned, reported on, and fixed whenever they're damaged. Reward team equipment managers with an appropriate bonus at the end of each year if they do a good job.

Designate a locked place to account for and secure the equipment. Not only will this deter people from stealing, but it also sends the message that the equipment is important and something to be respected.

ACTION STEP: Pick a leader to be a designated equipment manager who can be held accountable for the team's equipment and make an incentive program to offer encouragement.

MAINTENANCE

Equipment should be maintained at the end of each workday and not whenever work slows.

We've discovered it makes sense to hire a part- or full-time technician to carry out maintenance and repairs when the crew is done working. It beats paying employees overtime to do the job, especially when they're tired. Additionally, technicians are specially trained to fix equipment, whereas non-trained workers do a much less reliable job and take more time.

STEPPING STONE 4:
NEW JOB START-UP/JOB TURNOVER

NEW JOBS

Conduct Job Startup Meetings with new clients and key crew members to manage expectations and resolve questions and concerns.

Before the meeting give the landscape the doctor's equivalent of a "physical". Record what condition it's in, identify the areas where it needs help, and offer prescriptions to make it better.

Take written and photographic documentation of the existing conditions.

Making a record of pre-existing problems will prevent future disputes about how things looked before you began and will be a basis to show the progress of your work. Have the client view these documents and sign-off that he viewed them.

Go into the Job Startup Meeting with a check sheet so you don't forget to cover any bases.

We provide our Harvest Way Members with a Quality Counts Review sheet that covers the areas of landscape, turf, ornamentals, trees, irrigation, and general conditions. Once you and the client agree on the details and expectations of this review, you both should sign it so you have a clear agreement if you need to reference it in the future.

JOB TURNOVER

When you're turning a job back to the customer or another landscape company, cover your bases with a Job Turnover document. This document should review and score the site you've worked on and be signed by you and the client.

This will verify the job condition before it changes hands and protect you should any problems arise due to another maintenance handler's incompetence.

More importantly, we mention this step as a way to ensure you get paid for the work you've completed. Before you relinquish the job, be sure you've squared up any payments, as it can be difficult to get these taken care of after you leave.

STEPPING STONE 5: AG HORT

When it comes to using chemicals, fertilizers, and products, there are strict rules and regulations that differ from state to state and can result in hefty fines if not adhered to.

Make sure dangerous tools and products all have worksheets attached outlining how to use them, what safety equipment to wear, and any certifications or training that may be required.

Potentially dangerous chemicals such as fertilizer, gas, and poisons should be clearly labeled and have specific places for storage that are safe and clutter free.

Mark monthly calendar days to check in with the Agricultural Department, OSHA, suppliers, and online data sheets to make sure you're in compliance with any new laws regarding these chemicals and up-to-date with the latest, greatest, and most environmentally friendly options on the market.

When a crew member or members are assigned to use dangerous products, have them sign a document stating they've had the necessary training and give them a Personal Protection Equipment case after they've signed.

STEPPING STONE 6: QUALITY

Quality is one of those pop-marketing words that is over used, but seldom understood. Get it right and you'll reap the rewards of higher dividends and loyal customers. Get it wrong and you'll find your company wasting time repeating jobs and dealing with dissatisfied customers.

The trouble with quality is that it's subjective. When customers say they want a "quality job", the quality they're talking about depends on their individual expectations and requirements.

For example, quality to a residential customer is measured differently than quality to a corporate customer. For a corporate customer, quality might translate as a fast, reliable "no-excuses" service. But, for a residential customer, that same word might be used to refer to higher expectations of customer service and clean work attire.

The best way to maintain quality is to make it so it's not so much a guessing game by developing a grading system so you can measure it.

Create a list of the area you're landscaping (lawn, shrubs, trees, etc.) and rate each item on a 1-10 scale to represent levels of quality. Now, identify with your customer the specific levels of maintenance that equates to the appropriate numeric value on that scale. Maybe you're having a crew waste time pulling weeds when they should be spending more time meticulously trimming the grass.

With this list in hand, perform monthly inspections of a property aiming to meet or exceed the customer's expectations. You'll be able to determine which crews produce the best work and help improve the ones with low scores by focusing on the areas in which they're weak. This will allow you to develop stronger bench strength by partnering employees together to create better-balanced teams, where they can learn from each other's strengths and improve each other's weaknesses.

> **ACTION STEP:** Create a quality grading system for your most important properties and schedule a customer walk through.

STEPPING STONE 7: PRODUCTIVITY

What gets tracked or measured gets done. Set goals for the different stages of work your crew completes, i.e. showing up at the job site, being set-up for work, etc.

In our Harvest Way Guidebook "Profit Puzzle", we outline these stages in detail and provide exercises to help you train your crew to be more productive.

One of the big things we like to tell clients is to step back for a morning and observe how well your people operate, taking notes on how you can help improve their efficiency. Maybe they're losing time searching for materials or backing out trucks instead of having them lined up and ready to go. When it comes to traveling to a job, do the drivers have the best routes with regard to traffic patterns and heavy equipment pre-routed? When they get to a job site are crew members' tasks sequenced out or is it haphazard and left to chance?

Instead of looking to shave hours off the workday, aim for minutes. It's that old adage about eating an elephant one bite at a time. The minutes will add up.

STEPPING STONE 8: HORTICULTURE

This is the part of the business that got many of us hooked in the first place, the craft of taking care of plants. It helps to have a strong knowledge base to work from, which means being able to name and identify every plant on the property and knowing the ones that are working and the ones that are not.

Create a map of every job site and take a detailed plant inventory to show your customer at scheduled meetings. Many times, landscape plant designs are aesthetically pleasing, but the practicality side is lacking. Plants will die because they have shorter lifespans, were not planted correctly, or lack the right amount of sunlight or soil.

As a professional landscaper, it's your job to be able to quickly identify and know these reasons or have a knowledgeable worker who can.

There are a plethora of online resources, seminars, classes, and specialized agencies (NALP, TCIA, GCSSA, etc.) available to help you find the answers to any questions you have - it's just about being diligent enough to search.

OPERATIONS EXERCISES

This is a HUGE area and is in the BIG 4 category that we have mentioned before.

Just a little refresher on the BIG 4 -

#1: Find, Attract, Get On Board, Keep, and Grow the Right People

#2: Perform Consistently (This is what operations is all about!)

#3: Find, Attract, Get On Board, Keep, and Grow the Right Customers

#4: Make a Profit!

So, with this in mind, let's ask a few questions here:

- Take a good look at your safety program. What is your current WC Mod Rate? What are you currently paying for your worker's compensation insurance coverage per $100 of payroll? If this is too high, then it probably is a reflection on your safety record.

Action Step: Go back and build a better work safety program.

- How do you measure your quality, both internally and by external measures? How do you know, objectively, if you are meeting and exceeding your internal quality standards and more importantly your customers' standards?

Action Step: Build an Internal Quality Program. Tie it in with bonuses and wages.

- Take a good look at your job dispatch in the AM. Do your people get out in less than 8 minutes and are they ready to work? If not, what steps are needed to have a timely morning dispatch?
- Do you have formal NEW JOB START UP and JOB TURNOVER processes? If not, consider building these and use them religiously!
- What is the most innovative process, tool, piece of equipment, chemical, etc., that you have implemented in your business to make you more efficient, safe, and effective?

Action Step: Pick one area to focus on in the next season to improve your operations. Now, put this in writing and include who, what, when, how, and the plan for measuring the results.

Remember this -

"Change or be Changed – Changed Out!
Always adapt, change, and innovate."
The Harvesters

BUCKET #7: MARKETING

If you're fishing for new business, SALES is reeling the fish in and MARKETING is finding the right bait so the fish will bite.

Marketing is the message that attracts and prepares customers for the sale - advertising, public relations, branding, direct-mail, and social media are all found in this bucket.

The two main categories of marketing to pay attention to are how you promote your company and how customers interact and experience your company.

STEPPING STONE 1: MARKET RESEARCH

In this stage, you want to gather as much information as possible about who you will be marketing to, where those people are located, and why they should be interested in you. Don't worry about synthesizing yet, just collect.

DRIVE

An effective and old school way to find clients is by gaining a lay of the land - literally. Get out a map and draw a circle covering one hour's driving distance from your dispatch sites. Then, drive around, keeping an eye out for potential customers to pursue, recording who and where they are.

WEB SEARCH

Research the potential clients you've found online and look for other clients in the area you may have missed. Don't be shy to look at your competitors and whom they might be doing business with.

85

It's possible the landscape you saw during your drive was lacking maintenance and you can position yourself as the hero to swoop in and fix the problem.

DETAILS

Record details. Every detail you can collect on a potential customer, doesn't matter how trivial it may seem, record it. Even if the detail is an estimate, such as the general square footage of a site, the small parts will work together to create a larger plan helping you to determine the next course of action you should take.

> **ACTION STEP**: Draw a circle covering one hour's drive from a dispatch site and hit the pavement looking for potential customers.

STEPPING STONE 2: KNOW THYSELF

It's time for a SWOT analysis. Ask yourself specific questions about your Strengths, Weaknesses, Opportunities, and Threats. Take a few hours to write answers and conclusions for the categories. This exercise will give you a better understanding of your company.

STRENGTHS

- What victories did you enjoy last year?
- What jobs does your company perform best?
- What are your competitive advantages?

WEAKNESSES

- What areas do you struggle with (i.e. resources, people, Unique Selling Proposition)?
- Why do customers choose a competitor over you?
- What, if any, are your customer complaints?

OPPORTUNITIES

- Where can you grow your market?
- What other services can you offer customers?

- Are you taking advantage of technology to make your business more efficient?

THREATS

- Lawsuits
- Finances
- New legislation, etc.

For a SWOT worksheet and more detailed questions, check out our Marketing Bucket at the Harvest Way Academy.

STEPPING STONE 3: KNOW THY CUSTOMER

There are the customers you have and the customers you want to have. Before pursuing new ones, create files on the current ones you serve.

SITE VISIT

Upselling is a great source of new revenue. Visit all the properties you maintain at least once a year and consider how you might improve them. Even if customers don't purchase additional services, they will feel you are proactive and care. A favorable customer opinion will lead to an improved reputation and referrals.

ORGANIZE CUSTOMERS

Organize your customers by the segment they are in (residential, industrial, commercial, etc.) and then fill in details such as:

- How did you get them?
- Where are they located?
- How much do they spend?

Look for the Harvest Way Marketing Guidebook to get more ideas on how to research your customer.

Identify similarities amongst your current clients that will help you target new ones.

This list will also help you identify current customers who might not be worth the effort for the financial return. In these cases you may want to either increase their prices or amicably terminate the relationship. In this way crews can work on jobs with higher returns.

RESEARCH

Whatever details you're filling in, make sure to challenge all your assumptions. Guessing and half-baked assumptions will get you in trouble and can easily lead to lost profits.

> **ACTION STEP**: Choose one of your favorite customers to work for and brainstorm additional services you can offer.

STEPPING STONE 4: KNOW THY COMPETITION

Death and taxes . . . and, competition. In the landscape industry, there's always going to be competition, which is why you need to know your competitors.

Make a list of the top 3-5 companies that you compete with for jobs.

Visit each company's website, search public records, interview people who use the company, then write answers for the following questions:

- What market segment is your competitor in?
- What services and products does your competitor offer?
- What services and products doesn't your competitor offer?
- What are your competitor's strengths?
- What are your competitor's weaknesses?
- Where are the opportunities for your competitor?
- What are the threats for your competitor?

See: Harvestwayacademy.com/marketing-isnt-magic/
for more questions to ask about your competition.

When it comes to the businesses that your competitors serve, this information will help you position your company as the number two option in case the customers are ever unhappy.

STEPPING STONE 5: THE FOUR Ps - PRODUCTS, PRICING, PLACEMENT, PROMOTION

You can plan your marketing strategy using the FOUR Ps.

PRODUCTS

Make a list of the services and products you currently offer:

- Are there others you could be offering that customers want?
- Are there some you should stop offering or contract out?

PRICING

Your marketing people, who have an idea of what people want, what they're willing to pay for it, and what your competition is offering, will have a good pulse on how to price your services and products.

- Is there a formula or method for pricing? If not, write down how you previously priced work you've done.
- How long has it been since prices have been revised?
- What do competitors charge for similar services?
- Are you charging a higher gross margin for add-on work?

PLACEMENT

Look at the map you've drawn a circle on, marking an hour's radius from your office.

- Are you fully working within this radius?
- How are you reaching potential customers within this radius?
- Based on your target market, which geographical areas are best able to afford your services?
- Are there areas on the outskirts of the radius that might be worth expanding to?

PROMOTION

This is how you generate attention and get the word out about your company. Reflect upon the current ways you are promoting yourself and determine if your current promotions tie into your company brand and Unique Selling Proposition (USP).
(See STEPPING STONES 6 & 7 for more detail.)

STEPPING STONE 6: WHAT IS YOUR USP?

What makes you different than your competitors and what is your Unique Selling Proposition?

The answer to this question will give direction to how your company will position and promote its services.

Arriving at the answer takes a bit of soul searching.

A good way to discover your USP is by looking at your company culture, the services you offer, and the people you employ. Now, look at your competitors. If everyone is claiming to offer the same services, what is it about your company that stands out?

Once you pick a USP, follow through in making sure all aspects of your company contribute to that image.

For instance, if you want to be viewed as "the experts" in lawn care, offer incentives for your employees to educate themselves, contribute articles to the local paper, try to get radio spots on talk shows, speak at colleges - in other words, take actions that publicly reinforce your Unique Selling Proposition.

> **ACTION STEP:** Ask a few people on your sales team to repeat your company's USP. If they don't all say the same thing, it's time to get everyone on the same page.

STEPPING STONE 7:
ADVERTISING AND PROMOTION

This is how you get from where you are to where you want to go.

GET THE WORD OUT

Web marketing, direct mailing, advertising, knocking on doors, job site signs, attending trade shows, and public events are all ways to make people aware of your company.

Your company's soft advertising (uniforms, logo placement, colors, etc.) should be dialed in, too.

Tie these ad campaigns together with your company culture. For example, if your image is a "green" company, consider using recycled materials for your business cards.

BE DIFFERENT

Research how others are advertising and try to stand out in the customer's mind by being different.

Think of the GEICO gecko. There are tons of car insurance companies, but that charismatic little gecko differentiated GEICO enough to increase its market share by 2%.

Use planned advertising campaigns to separate your business from the "field of sameness".

SOCIAL MARKETING

Social marketing allows you to engage with a high volume of customers and prospects. Videos, photos, and social media sites like Facebook, Instagram, Twitter, and LinkedIn are key to building a presence online.

All your promotions should be aimed at generating curiosity to get people to visit your website by making them want to find out more about your company. Find experts in the field and make sure your website and social media presences are current, accurate, and compelling.

INTEGRATED MARKETING

It's usually not the case that one specific promotion will get people calling, but rather an integrated marketing program that will bring results. For example, queue direct mailing campaigns with news and radio ads, billboards, and whatever other advertising methods you're able to whip up.

Be aware of your target audience. Some tactics, such as direct mail, will work better on residential customers, but have little effect on commercial ones.

Consider bringing in an expert as you could waste a lot of time and money by not promoting correctly.

STEPPING STONE 8: CUSTOMER TOUCH POINTS

Customer touch points are the way people will interact and experience your company, shaping favorable or unfavorable opinions about it.

PHONE

Receptionist – By far the best option for answering calls. Make sure the receptionist sounds pleasant, gives a name, and follows a greeting script that echoes your USP and company culture.

Voicemail – Record a short, friendly, and positive message. Ask if you can hear the smile of the person in the recording.

Return Calls – Return all calls in a timely manner. If an email or another interaction might be interpreted negatively, make a phone call or meet in person to clear things up.

WEB

Email – Have the company logo on all emails and a relevant quote or slogan to reinforce your brand. ALWAYS proof emails before sending.

Website – At least twice a year compare your website with your competitors. Does your site make it easy for clients to find what they're looking for? Bring in a professional to help with Search Engine Optimization (SEO) to bolster your online presence. Make sure your brand and colors are visible and consistent throughout every page.

Social Media – This can quickly turn into a full-time job. Consider delegating the responsibility to a tech savvy employee or an outside company to engage in online forums, update, and post to social media sites and look for new opportunities for business.

PROJECTS

Proposals – Find out who the decision maker in the company is and do your best to get the proposal into his/her hands (See SALES BUCKET – Stepping Stone 6: Proposals and Follow-up).

Invoices – Make sure these are sent within a timely manner. Some companies include marketing messages on invoices for their customers to consider.

PEOPLE

Outfits – The way your employees dress reflect upon your company. Make sure there is a consistent dress code and color scheme for brand consistency.

Conduct – Every time a person interacts with you or your employees they form an opinion. A positive work environment stems from your company culture and how you treat your employees.

Conflict Resolution – Complaints are going to happen. Look at them as an opportunity to improve your company and forge a stronger bond between you and your customers.

BUCKET #8:
SALES

Closing sales allows your company to thrive. Fail to make new sales and your yearly harvest of profit will be lean.

"Sales" is part of the marketing process and not the other way around.

This is the activity where you or your salespeople have meetings, make phone calls, network, and meet with prospective customers to sell a service or product.

In the landscaping business there are two types of salespeople:

1) Order Takers – follow up on leads that come into the office.

2) Business Developers – go into new territory and cultivate potential customers.

Regardless of which type of sales people are doing, it's important to always track the progress every step of the way - from leads, to proposals, to contracts - so you know which areas you need to improve.

STEPPING STONE 1: GAME PLAN

Not having a sales Game Plan is like tossing a Hail Mary every time you pitch your company. It doesn't matter how long you've been in business, you need to develop a strategy for setting goals, targeting which customers you want to find, defining who these customers are, and how you will approach them.

SET GOALS

Discuss with management what your sales goals are for the company before each new season.

Examples of such goals might be: How many proposals would you like to achieve every month? What is the minimum and maximum each proposal could be for? What jobs/clients do you want to win? Etc.

Your goals should tie into your marketing plan.

For a list of goals we usually recommend our clients to set, see the Harvest Way Sales Guidebook at: Harvestwayacademy.com/files/guidebooks/HarvestWay-Sales-Guidebook.pdf

PRIORITIZE CUSTOMERS

Your time is valuable.

If you start putting 100% effort into every potential lead, you'll have no time to run your business. Be tactical about whom you're researching and approaching.

1) Make a list of your customers from your most lucrative to your least profitable.

2) Fill in specifics about each customer to determine why they rank where they do.

3) Identify the top 200 jobs within your selected territory, collecting basic information such as location, size, approximate worth, etc.

4) Rank potential clients that share traits with your most lucrative ones.

Check out Harvestwayacademy.com/files/tools/HWA_SalesTouches.pdf for a comprehensive guide on how to research and rank potential customers.

PLAN YOUR APPROACH

In the same way you wouldn't go deer hunting in the ocean, you should know who your clients are before you approach them.

- Who is the decision maker for each account?
- Is the account involved in any outside charities or events you can attend?
- Does the account use an outside management company?
- Do you have any connections to the top decision maker?

If they already have a landscape service, figure out who your competitor is and position yourself as the number two option.

ACTION STEP: After finding the top 200 jobs in your territory, thoroughly research only the ones that are within an hour from your work location and write out a plan of approach.

STEPPING STONE 2: PROSPECTING & QUALIFYING

Finding new clientele is a lot like drilling for oil - you have to know where to drill and if there's enough profit in the ground to make it worth drilling for.

PROSPECTING

There are plenty of ways to mine potential clients - cold calling, newspapers, your network of employees and vendors, trade shows, etc.

Once you've built a healthy database of potential clients, it's time to start narrowing it down by setting standards for your company.

1) Identify the jobs you want over the next 3-5 years. (Don't be shy about asking your account managers which accounts might be desirable.)

2) Focus on the "premier" jobs that are an hour or less from your dispatch area or 15 minutes from existing job sites.

3) Does the job have long-term potential and room for upgrades?

4) Do recon on your target customers and find out as much as you can before approaching.

QUALITY

It's about working smarter, not harder. Having good client selection is one of the most direct ways a company can increase its profits, reduce stress, and better serve its customers.

Once you've targeted and researched your clients, it's time to make contact and ask qualifying questions to determine if you and your potential customer will be a good match.

Develop a qualifying list of questions by writing down characteristics of the good and bad clients you have worked with. Now you can begin ranking both your new and existing clients on each question and assign them a grade like, "A", "B", "C", "D".

The same questions should be applied to potential clients that have contacted you.

At the end of each conversation, tally up the client's GPA (grade point average) to decide if the client is worth investing your time.

> **ACTION STEP**: Write a list of Qualifying Questions to ask potential clients.

STEPPING STONE 3: CONTACT

Now that you've narrowed down "who" to contact, it's time to focus on "how".

THE GATEKEEPER

This is the person who keeps time-wasters from getting through to the boss. It's a good practice to be friendly and honest with gatekeepers and not try to sneak past them.

If you don't have any names to drop, it usually takes a few calls to convince them to put you through.

These people can be a source of information when it comes to determining things like who the head decision maker is in the company.

ANSWERING THE PHONE

Whether a person is returning a call you solicited or is calling you for the first time, it's important to do your best to always have a person answer the phone.

Answering services are a solution, but are usually not very good. A better solution is to hire a virtual assistant who works from home or have calls screened and try to take every important one yourself.

The next best option is to have a voicemail that immediately sends you the message. If you're choosing this option, be sure to call potential clients back as soon as possible as it reflects poorly on your service to keep a person waiting.

LEAD SHEETS

However you decide to answer the phone, make sure to fill out a "Lead Sheet" for every new caller.

This sheet has basic information like:

- Contact info
- Why the person called
- How they heard of you
- Their pain points

FIRST PHONE APPOINTMENT

If a gatekeeper puts you through - be ready. If it's a call back, be on time with your appointment.

This is your chance to speak with the decision maker and give a proposal to win the contract. Make sure you've studied the company's landscape, know who your competitors are, and how you can help that person's business to look better or save money.

You may only get one chance to talk so make sure you have a compelling reason for the decision maker to listen.

FIRST IN-PERSON MEETING

Always confirm your appointments and be sure to be on time. Use the person's name, shake his/her hand, and be sure to smile!

Use the first few minutes to exchange cordialities and build rapport by trying to find commonalities with them. However, don't blab on too long as these people don't have a lot of time.

When you get down to business your initial conversation should aim to discover the client's "pain points" by asking what problems the client is having. Ask questions that show you've done your research and listen carefully, allowing the other person to do most of the talking.

At the end of your conversation, be clear about what the next step will be, i.e. who is going to do what and when. Get an agreement and then do what you promise.

Follow up the meeting with a "thank you" note, with your company's logo.

STEPPING STONE 4: ESTIMATING

If you want to turn a profit, you need to know what price points to charge and KNOW YOUR COSTS!

In the maintenance business, the main costs in estimating are the man-hours and materials needed to complete the job.

LABOR

- Costs about 25-50% of your revenue.
- Includes number of workers per job, their hourly wage, plus extras like health insurance, 401k, etc.
- TIP: Scout out the current contractor or look at jobs you have that might be similar to determine how much manpower you'll need.

MATERIALS

- Costs about 6-25% of your revenue, with costs increasing with the more enhancements and installations you promise.
- Tools, fertilizers, chemicals, seeds, new/rental equipment.
- Have a clear idea of the size of the job you will be working on to estimate the amount of materials.

JOB SITE

- Visit the job site.
- Estimate how long it takes to travel there.
- Define the boundary lines and size of the job.

DON'T FORGET

- Put your estimate in writing and keep a record of it.
- Whose specifications are being used for the estimate, yours or the customer's?
- What are the frequencies of the tasks?
- What will the job cleanup be like, i.e. Are trash bins included or do you need to bring your own?
- Consider the surroundings:
    - What is the irrigation system like and what irrigation needs do you have?

- o Are there hedges, balconies, etc.?
- o Are there times of day/night when you're not allowed to work?

Get a more in-depth look at estimating guidelines and methods at Harvestwayacademy.com/files/guidebooks/HarvestWay-Estimating-Guibebook.pdf

STEPPING STONE 5: PRICING

Having the right price will allow you to turn a profit while remaining competitive in the marketplace.

GET THE RIGHT PRICE

At the core of finding the right price will be your estimate.

Once you have a detailed estimate of what it will take to get a job done, markup the estimate to account for overhead costs of running your company and a fair net profit.

Determining how much to markup will depend on the marketplace, what competitors are charging for similar jobs, and the value customers perceive they will be getting from your company.

You don't need to be the lowest priced option, but you do want customers to believe they're getting good value for their money.

Make sure you're consistently delivering your services at a level that meets or exceeds your customer's expectations. Keep an eye on your Gross Margin, always looking for ways to keep costs down while working more efficiently without sacrificing quality.

PRICE INFLUENCERS

The Marketplace – Know who your top competitors are and get an idea of how much they're charging for similar jobs. Keep your rates within 10-15% of the competition.

<u>Pay Rates</u> – Competitive pay wages might make costs slightly higher but it's worth the extra investment to reduce turnover and novice blunders.

<u>Perceived Value</u> – Learn what your customer perceives as value, other than price, and focus on marketing these aspects of your company.

<u>Market Density/Location</u> – The location of the job will override its size. You will save money if it's closer to other existing job sites. If there is little competition in the area, you can get a better price for your work.

<u>Smart Purchasing</u> – Buy smart and in bulk to lower your costs. Suppliers will often give discounts if you pay on time.

<u>Supervision Ratios</u> - Size, location, difficulty, and nature of the job will influence the ratio of required supervisors to workers. High-end residential projects require a higher ratio than large industrial projects. Know your needed ratios and price accordingly.

PRICE TACTICS AND STRATEGY

- Review public work bids submitted by your competition. These are public record.
- Perform lost jobs debriefs. Customers are more likely to share what position you came in and will tell you if you came in too high or too low of the awarded price.
- Find out who got the job and keep track of the information.
- Compare with friendly competitors. You don't always need to be transparent, but building friendly relationships with competitors will allow you to get a better feel for the marketplace.
- Determine some net profit ranges of the job you're pricing out: Break even scenario, 1-5% net profit, 5-10% net profit, 10-15% net profit, or even more, depending on the project.

For videos, formulas, worksheets, and more information on how to arrive at the right price, see Harvestwayacademy.com/the-price-is-right-2/

ACTION STEP: Identify who your top competitors are and compare your prices and services on similar jobs. Are your prices within 10-15%? If not, what are the reasons?

STEPPING STONE 6: PROPOSAL AND FOLLOW-UP

An invitation to write a proposal is a milestone in the sales cycle, and the final hurdle before closing.

Most of your competition will deliver standard proposals. If you can outshine them in this stage, you stand a much better chance of winning the job.

HOW TO PREPARE

1) Know the due date and level of proposal a job expects - ranging from a short informal proposal to a deluxe one that includes written documents, visual aids, and a meeting.

2) Walk through the job site (hopefully, with the customer) and have a clear understanding of the customer's current situation, pain points, and expectations of your company.

3) Research specific details:

    a.   Company history/company culture
    b. Names of employees
    c.   Size of job

4) Identify 3-5 things you can do to improve your customer's business.

5) Determine the customer's main motivation for seeking a proposal.

6) Determine what the client is willing to pay, so you'll know if it's worth your time to write a proposal.

WHAT TO WRITE

A great proposal begins by highlighting the problem(s) a client is facing and how it impacts the client's business.

People buy results.

Before you dive into the details of how you're going to execute a project, make sure you clearly state the concrete goals.

Keep in mind that you're not writing an estimate. An estimate provides a price quote and keeps the client focused on price. A proposal provides a summary of a client's problems and keeps the client focused on the value they'll receive when you come to help.

Be generous with your ideas.

Organize the proposal exactly as the client requests or in the order you think the client would find the most appropriate.

Don't conclude with a price for the job. Conclude by stating the terms and including a call to action, i.e. "Send this page back, signed and dated, and we can commence immediately!"

FORMATING

- Sweat every detail!
- Use high quality materials, i.e. paper, folders, pens, etc., with the logo and brand consistency of your company.
- Spell names and titles right.
- Use headings and page numbers, which you can easily refer to in a meeting.
- Keep it short. Proposals less than 5 pages in length are 31% more likely to win   business.
- The Executive Summary should not be more than a page in length.
- Use simple words.
- Use easily understood graphics. It should not take longer than 10 seconds to know what the graphic means.

DELIVERY

Be on time delivering your proposal.

Try your best to deliver the proposal face-to-face. This gives a sense of your company's personality, culture, and passion. Try to dress similarly to your client as this sort of mirroring helps build rapport.

Always be prepared to give a presentation, even if it's not expected.

If you're using an agreement form, have your portion signed before handing it over. Likewise, if you are required to use a client's form, check with your attorney on the contract wording before signing.

Have extra copies of your proposal ready in case there are more people in the room.

FOLLOW-UP

Be clear in your proposal when you are going to follow-up. Don't wait for them to contact you!

There are hundreds of books on how to write a good proposal. When it comes to the landscape industry, the Harvest Way Academy, Harvestwayacademy.com/killer-proposals/, has proposal writing materials that will take your presentation to the next level.

STEPPING STONE 7: CLOSING

Closing sales is about trust. While a great proposal will inspire and build this trust, there are other actions you can take that will help to seal the deal.

MIRRORING

The strength of a handshake, the attire a person wears, the tone of voice, posture, etc. - Studies show the more you subtly reflect another's characteristics, the more that person will feel bonded to you.

SMILE AND LISTEN

Be an active listener. When you're done presenting, let the client do 75% of the talking while you smile. If you don't agree with something, smiling is even more important! A smile says you are on the same team and want to work together to figure out a solution.

BE PREPARED

Being prepared for the unexpected obstacles that might arise displays foresight, confidence, and capability. Some examples of this are showing up early and always having a pen and extra proposals on hand.

LEAVE NO QUESTIONS

Make sure you've answered all questions in a meeting by saying something like, "Do you have everything you need to make a decision?" If you don't know the answer, find it out immediately and get back to them as fast as you can. Unanswered questions create doubt.

TESTIMONIALS

A testimonial booklet with photos and quotes by other satisfied clients is a great way to show you have a track record of success and that your company is reliable. Leave a testimonial pamphlet at the end of the meeting and put quotes from satisfied customers up on your website.

SCHEDULE A FOLLOW-UP

Following up is a way of telling your client, "I care about your business." Ask if it's okay to check in after a few days and suggest a time and date.

STEPPING STONE 8: HAND OFF

Handing off a signed contract to your managers is like landing a plane. You want the transition to go smoothly.

An efficient and successful way to do this is to hold a New Project meeting before work commences and try to get the customer to attend the meeting. This sends the message that you are serious about doing a great job and will give you the opportunity to introduce your key people, brief both parties on what to expect, and resolve any questions and concerns.

If the big boss does attend, don't waste time covering small details unless he/she wants to hear them.

Use the meeting as a way to introduce your team and learn as much about the customer as possible.

At the close, schedule subsequent meetings to make sure expectations are being met. These meetings are a great opportunity to learn more about the people you're working with, present invoices, accept checks, and review change orders.

For large jobs, try to have three tiers of management from both sides in attendance. This way, if someone on either side leaves their position or gets promoted, there will be other points of contact and familiarity.

Sometimes, when a new manager takes over a job, the manager might bring in a vendor he/she already knows. This will put the future of your contract in jeopardy. Having scheduled meetings will reduce the chances of this happening.

Establish a single contact person for the job in case the customer has suggestions, questions, or concerns.

People have short-term memories. Take before and after pictures when you begin and end a job. This will allow you to show the customer that hiring your company was a smart decision.

ACTION STEP: If you don't already have one, make a system for filing the "before and after" pictures on your computer, of these new job sites.

SALES EXERCISES

Always remember - "Nothing Happens without a Sale!" Head Harvester Ed

Ask yourself and take action on these keys to sales success.

- Do you have a Sales Game Plan in place? Is it in writing? Does it have goals specifically spelled out? How often is it reviewed? Who is involved?

- How many customer testimonials do you have? List them. Are they current and fresh? Do they address the pain points you solved that are similar to new potential customers' pain points? Go get 10-15 new testimonials. Try to get these on video or, at the very least, audio. Remember: Your best salesperson is a happy, completely satisfied customer.

- Do you have an estimating program that can be universally understood and used by more than one person? If not, build one or buy one.

- Identify the top 200 clients you want to do business with and build your plan to reach these customers.

- Take a good look at the proposals that you submit to your potential customers. Do these REALLY DIFFERENTIATE you from the rest of the crowd or are you just running in the same pack? Make them more relational and less transactional. Go for the heart and the emotions! Use lots of photos of their property to build your compelling case to select your company.

- Build a customer selection criteria process to help determine the key indicators to go forward with a prospect or to hold your horses for continuing your pursuit of a customer. What are the must haves from a desired customer? What are the RED flags that will tell you not to go after them? Get these in place and it will make it a whole lot easier to get the RIGHT customer from the start.

- Know the top 10 most common objections and have some awesome positive and unique rebuttals. Practice these positive and professional rebuttals to PERFECTION. List the top 10, begin your rebuttals building, and practice, practice, practice!

- How does the handoff from sales to operations work at your organization? Build a formal process and MAKE CERTAIN the customer is handled professionally right from the start. Make a personal visit to the owner, salesperson, or the top operations person and do a simple survey to verify you got off to a great start!

Conclusion

Okay, there you have it. Whether you're just starting a business or a veteran, we're sure all of this information has given you plenty to think about and hopefully act on. Remember, as they say, "Rome wasn't built in a day" and neither are landscape companies.

One of the keys to success from our experience is to make a complete list of everything that needs to be done. Then, from this list, prioritize everything into three separate lists - Urgent, Important, and Long Term. Next, take the top three items from each of the lists and put them on top of each of the lists. By accomplishing these items first you will leverage the greatest positive impact on your company.

The question all owners ask us at this point is, "Where am I going to find time to do all these things?"

If you are working every day in the field, then it will be difficult, but not impossible. If this is the case, you may have to block an hour or so in the evenings or on weekends to get these things done. If you are out of the direct operations of your company then you can block time during the week. Even if you work on these items one hour every other day, at the end of a month much will be accomplished. One thing for sure, the only way extremely busy people get things done is by scheduling the time they need in their calendar and doing the best they can not to let anything interfere.

Our final thought before ending is this, create a vision of where you're going. Do you want a $1M, $2M, $5M, $10M, or $20M company? Will you work in residential or commercial markets or both? Geographically, what is the radius and/or distance you want to travel? As Stephen Covey said in his book, *7 Habits of Highly Successful People*, begin with the end in mind. Just write down what you think your vision is, not to worry, you can change it, but just write it down for starters. Now, work toward fulfilling this vision every day. Set goals for the month, the quarter, the year, and little by little you will put the pieces to the puzzle together and, before you know it, your vision will be accomplished.

One thing for sure though, make sure you take care of your family and yourself. It's awesome to work hard but you also need to have fun along the way. Be sure to continue to be curious about things and keep asking why things are being done the way they are. Learn all you can about every aspect of your work. Visit other non-competing companies. Keep looking for ways to improve everything, every day.

The Harvesters hope this book will help in your quest and, if you need further help, we want you to know we are all here to help you ... *Harvest Your Potential.*

Join The Harvest Way Academy

An online resource to learn the business of landscaping.

- Feel stuck not knowing how to get more quality employees
- Want to take your company to the next level
- Need organizational process in your company.

Grow your business faster, make more money and reduce the possibility of mistakes with landscape business training by joining The Harvest Way Academy.

Whether your Green Industry Business is in: Maintenance, Design Build, Installation, Construction, Tree Care, Plantscapes or Lawn Care…

You will learn how to:

- Be More Competitive
- Grow Your Company
- Find and Hire the Right People
- Keep the Right Customers
- Close More Sales
- Learn New Strategies

The Harvesters cover every aspect of your business and deliver content by:

- Educational Lessons on Video
- Downloadable Guidebooks
- Useful Tools and Handouts
- Virtual Workshops and Webinars
- Regular Emails to Keep you Motivated

LEARN	GROW	PROFIT
1	2	3
Watch Our Video Lessons, Work The Tools	Apply The Business Skills You've Learned	Make Money In All Market Conditions!

**Build a Successful Landscape Business
Without Working Yourself into the Ground**

Popular courses include:

- The Basics and Fundamentals of Estimating
- Develop Your Pricing Tactics and Strategies
- Using Market Research and Finding Customer Potential
- Executing a Winning Profit Plan
- Prepare Your Company to Sell From the Beginning

To learn more and start

your $10 trial offer, visit:

HarvestWayAcademy.com

Consider The
Harvest Leaders Group

Have you ever asked yourself...

- What's stopping me from taking my business to the next level?
- Who can I talk to confidentially about my business?
- How do I get fresh innovative ideas and systems implemented for my business?
- I feel so overwhelmed at times do other owners feel the same way?
- I have no one to compare my financials with and my CPA doesn't get it.

This is where the Harvest Leaders Group (HGL) can really benefit you. You will join a group of non-competing owners who have similar goals as you, make more money with less stress, have more free time and enjoy the process.

HLG will create a personal learning plan and be held accountable. There is complete confidentiality within the group and that's why members become a "Circle of Trust" all working together to positively impact your business and your life!

The group becomes your sounding board. You will overcome owner isolation yet will with the opportunity to be yourself and be understood.

Without a doubt such a group will help improve your odds of success. You will make fewer mistakes and progress with your goals 10 times faster than you could have by yourself.

The Harvest Leaders Group may be just for you!

- Helps you overcome owner's isolation
- Provides you a place and an opportunity to be yourself
- Becomes your sounding board for problem solving
- Participation will improve your odds of success
- You get to work with similar people from similar organization

Who is the facilitator of these groups?

Harvester Fred Haskett with over 40 years of experience in the Green Industry. He started by building his own $3 million dollar residential maintenance company in 1980, sold that and moved on to roles with The Brickman Group and ValleyCrest Companies franchise subsidiary, US Lawns. Fred managed over $45 million of business annually. He's got an LIC certification of NALP, a certified turf grass professional from PLCAA and is a certified arborist through ISA.

Now this isn't just another "peer group," Harvester Fred will be collaborating with the other Harvesters and they will be working with the groups as well.

If you are curious go to:

HarvestLeadersGroup.com

or Contact Fred Haskett directly at

Fred@HarvestLandscapeConsulting.com

or by phone at **(619) 665-7854**

The Harvest
Leaders Group

Rely on Expertise to Help your Human Resources Program

Everyone knows the world of human resources is becoming increasingly complex. Instead of getting frustrated by this web of forms, laws, and bureaucracy, the Harvest Group provides clear expertise in this area that will allow you to maintain legal compliance and build an effective human resources program that will allow you to get running your company!

Head Harvester for Human Resources, Steve Cesare, Ph.D. has over 30 years of human resources experience to help you achieve that goal.

Employee Handbooks

At a time when human resources laws are requiring companies to revise their policies to maintain compliance, a well-designed employee handbook can serve as an invaluable resource to many administrative, operational, and managerial decisions. Employee handbooks should be reviewed and revised annually to ensure their content remains current, efficient, and tailored to the company's business goals.

Performance Management

Employee issues like discipline, conflict resolution, and termination take up a lot of time. With the constant threat of discrimination, wrongful termination, or retaliation present at every step of the human resources program, it is imperative that your company institute a performance management system that holds employees accountable for their actions, while doing so in a legal manner.

Recruitment and Staffing

Companies are always looking for qualified employees who will help them achieve their business goals. A proper staffing plan including recruitment, orientation, and on-boarding is critical employee retention in terms of saving time, money, and effort in attracting, developing, training, and retaining key employees on your team regardless of their position.

Employment Laws

Whether it is I-9 Forms, overtime, or interviewing, the number of employment laws affects almost every aspect of your company and its human resources programs. Given the number and complexity of these changes laws, and the fines associated with them, it is certainly in your best interest to know how to direct your business legally, efficiently, and profitably.

Additional services include the following HR areas:

- Employee Safety
- Strategic Planning
- Employee Relations
- Compensation
- Change Management
- Training and Development

Take a proactive, and results-oriented approach to solve your HR problems

A professional approach to human resources can significantly help a company differentiate itself from business competitors. That competitive advantage can lead to reduced legal liability, improved efficiency, and long-term success. Steve Cesare, can help you with all aspects of your company's employee issues.

Steve Cesare, PhD., Head Harvester for HR

steve@harvestlandscapeconsulting.com

760-685-3800

How Else Can The Harvesters Help My Company?

If you want to take your business to the next level,
our seasoned, Green Industry Experts can help you!

Company Assessments

Perhaps you may be interested in obtaining an in depth on site
assessment of your company that includes a short and long term
action plan.

"One to One" Coaching/Consulting

Or, you may be interested in exploring "one to one" coaching with
the ability to seek advice from a Harvester on a more personal
basis. If this is the case contact Harvester Bill on the West Coast or
Harvest Ed on the East Coast and they would be happy to talk about
how they can help.

"In-House" Training Seminars

The Harvesters can also provide seminars for your sales team,
account managers or your entire management staff. These may be
half day or all day sessions. Ask us about a tailor made program to
accomplish your needs.

Talks, Seminars, Keynote Addresses

Harvesters, Bill, Ed, Steve & Fred provide a variety of topics for
various venues. They have delivered discourses and training both
domestically and internationally for privet, state and national
organizations. For a complete list for each please visit:
harvestlandscapeconsulting.com.

Get unstuck and on the right track

- Grow your landscape business and increase your profit
- Find, train and keep the right people
- Create a Sustainable, Money-Making company
- Learn strategies to make running your business easier

Learn more on how The Harvest Group

can help you and your business

HarvestLandscapeConsulting.com

The Harvest Group Products

**GREEN SIDE UP - Straight Talk on Growing
and Operating a profitable Landscape Business**
By Ed Laflamme

Paperback - Second Edition

Ed's book is an idea farm, an easy-to-follow guide
to cultivating a successful land care business.

**GREEN SIDE UP - Straight Talk on Growing
and Operating a profitable Landscape Business**
By Ed Laflamme

7 CD Set, Audio Book - First Edition

Harvest Recruiting Kit
by Bill Arman

Proven Landscape Industry Tips, Tactics &
Techniques for Finding and Getting "On Board"
The Right People Includes: Book, Workbook,
Video Series & Toolb

The Harvester Bios

BILL ARMAN

Bill Arman is a 40-year green industry veteran, 2006 National Landscape Leadership Award recipient, and author of the book and recruiting kit, *"The Harvest Way for Recruiting and Hiring the Right People."*

Upon graduating from Cal Poly - San Luis Obispo with a BS in Ornamental Horticulture, he joined ValleyCrest Companies. During his nearly 30-year career with ValleyCrest Companies, Bill worked his way through many field positions, culminating as Regional Vice President for Southern California, overseeing a $25 million portfolio with six offices, five separate service lines, and 600 project sites with over 700 employees.

Bill has worked with some of the most prestigious projects nationally and locally in Southern California, including nine Ritz Carlton locations nationwide, South Coast Plaza, Nixon Library, University of La Verne, Cal Baptist University, Texas Tech, The Mission Inn, the Irvine Company, and the Fairplex, to name but a few.

While at ValleyCrest, Bill also spent two years as VP of Human Resources, serving as the primary architect for the development and implementation of the national training program, performance management system, and the recruiting program for this 10,000 employee company.

In the fall of 2007, Bill co-founded a national landscape business consultancy/coaching firm called The Harvest Group, where he serves as The Head Harvester. The Harvest Group serves clients in 45 states and 5 countries, ranging in size from $100,000 to $50,000,000 in annual revenue.

"Head Harvester" Bill now lives his true-life purpose and passion in "Harvesting the Potential" of organizations and individuals throughout the Western United States, Canada, South Africa, and India.

bill@harvestlandscapeconsulting.com • 949-466-8837

STEVE CESARE, Ph.D.

Steve Cesare has more than 30 years of human resources experience. Currently, Steve is a Principal Consultant with The Harvest Group, a nationwide firm, with four regional offices, emphasizing improved organizational performance through human resources, business operations, and customer relations management. Prior to joining The Harvest Group, Steve was employed with Bemus Landscape, Jack in the Box, the County of San Diego, Citicorp, Sentara Health Systems, and NASA.

Steve earned his Ph.D in Industrial/Organizational Psychology from Old Dominion University. He has authored 51 professional journal articles and made 43 presentations at professional conferences.

Additionally, he has 17 years of collegiate teaching experience at Old Dominion University and the University of San Diego where he taught in the Departments of Psychology, Business, and the MBA program.

As a strategic business partner, Steve's areas of direct value include helping clients with their employee handbooks, performance management programs, compensation systems, training and development, safety and worker's compensation, and wage and hour issues.

steve@harvestlandscapeconsulting.com • 760-685-3800

CINDY CODE

For nearly 30 years, Cindy Code has been asking questions, touring landscape companies, writing about best business practices and interviewing awesome entrepreneurs.

Earning a journalism degree from Ohio University's E.W. Scripps School of Journalism, Cindy found a home in the landscape industry. Starting as an intrepid reporter and editor for *Lawn & Landscape* magazine, she earned her reputation as an in-depth writer – exploring the ins and outs of leading lawn and landscape businesses.

In her roles as editor, account manager, publisher and Internet content manager, Cindy earned a reputation as a respected journalist, communicator and active participant within the industry. She served on the boards of numerous state and national associations, attended conferences and trade shows regionally and nationwide and traveled anywhere the story took her.

Along the way, Cindy's path inevitably crossed with both Ed and Bill and they began working together writing books, presenting seminars and hosting the podcast program, "The Grow Show." As a Harvester, Code works with landscape companies on their marketing and communications plans as well as leads the Customer Counts program.

She is an award-winning journalist honored by the Turf & Ornamental Communicators Association, the American Society of Business Press Editors and the Cleveland Press Club for her numerous contributions to the field. In addition to her specialization on landscape industry PR, website content, e-newsletters and customer service, Code is an advocate and promoter of the benefits of yards, parks and green spaces in her role as Executive Director of Project EverGreen.

cindy@harvestlandscapeconsulting.com • 440-463-6445

FRED HASKETT

For over 40 years Fred Haskett has been growing businesses in the "Green Industry". After leaving Ohio State University in 1977, he first worked in a small local Garden Center for a few years until he founded a Residential Lawn Care Company in his home town of Dover, Ohio. For ten years, he grew GreenWorld Lawn & Landscape Management from a one man-one truck operation in 1980 into a Multi-Faceted firm with revenues of 2 million, providing Residential Lawn & Tree Care and Full Service Commercial Landscape Maintenance by 1990.

Since 1990 Fred has had the opportunity to work as a senior leader with some of the most outstanding organizations in the Green Industry - The J C Ehrlich Green Team, The Brickman Group, The Valley Crest Companies, U S Lawns, and most recently Landscape Development, Inc. in Valencia, CA. He has served as President, Vice President, Regional Manager and Division Manager and has had P&L responsibility for Multi State / Multi Branch operations with revenues exceeding $45 Million annually. During his career Fred has directly managed the sales and production of over $70 million in lawn care and tree care services and $ 180 million landscape services.

As Head Harvester, with the Harvest Landscape Consulting Group, Fred coaches and consults with owners of small, medium, and large Lawn Care, Tree Care and Landscape companies. He loves the Green Industry and the people in it. Today, he spends his time helping folks like you, *"Harvest your Potential"* by developing new methods to properly manage and lead a successful enterprise.

Fred has had extensive experience in several areas of the "Green Industry" Including Residential Lawn and Tree Care Operations, Full Service Commercial Landscape Management, Design Build, Arbor Care, Water Management, and Snow and Ice Removal. In addition, he has extensive experience in Franchise System operation and development. He is a *"Landscape Industry Certified Manager"* thru the "National Association of Landscape Professionals (NALP), a *"Certified Turf Grass Professional"* thru the "University of Georgia" and a *"Certified Arborist"* thru the "International Society of Arboriculture" (ISA).

In support of the Green Industry, Fred currently serves on the Board of Directors of Project Evergreen and on the Government Affairs and Lawn Care Specialty Committee's for the "National Association of Landscape Professionals" (NALP) a national organization of over 4,000 Lawn and Landscape Companies. Previously he has served three terms on the Board of Directors of NALP and two terms as Chairman of the Lawn Care Specialty Group. In addition, he has been on the Advisory Board of "Landscape Management" Magazine and has written a monthly blog for the publication

In 2006 Fred was honored by his peers by being named a *TRAILBLAZER* for Lifetime Green Industry Achievement by the "National Association of Landscape Professionals".

A published Author, Fred wrote "CONTAINMENT SYSTEMS DESIGN" A guidebook for chemical storage, mixing and recycling. Published in 1995 by Advanstar. In addition, he has written articles for *Lawn and Landscape Turf Lawn Care Industry and Landscape Management"* magazines" Since 1989 he has been a speaker at dozens of National and State meetings and Conferences. Fred also served for three years on the Seminar Faculty of the Golf Course Superintendents Association of America.

Fred and his wife Kelly divide their time between Port Hueneme, CA aboard their 36' sailboat Touché and their home in a small town in Missouri, called Lake St Louis. They spend their leisure time sailing in the Caribbean and Pacific, chasing their seven grandchildren, intruding into their two children's lives, and trying to break 100 on the golf course.

fred@harvestlandscapeconsulting.com • 619-665-7854

ALISON A. HOFFMAN

Alison has more than 25 years of experience in strategy, operations, mergers and acquisitions and delivering business-to-business client solutions. Her areas of expertise include managing operations for profitable growth, organizational design and strategy activation. She brings a wealth of experience through her work in evaluating, valuing and purchasing over 30 companies, leading company-wide cultural and business integration projects and consolidating best practices among business processes and corresponding computing systems. Over the last two decades, she has led over 100 projects spanning acquisition screening, company valuation, due diligence and mergers and acquisitions advisory services.

Alison is a founding member of Harvest the Green Partners. Prior to joining Harvest the Green Partners, Alison started and ran her own garden design and consulting firm. Previous to that, she served as Senior Vice President of Mergers and Acquisitions for a NYSE U. S. financial services and human resource consulting firm. Alison received her Master in Business Administration from Southern Methodist University in Dallas and completed her BA at University of Pittsburgh. She is a member of the Association for Corporate Growth and the International Business Brokers Association, Inc.

Alison@harvestlandscapeconsulting.com • 224-688-8838

ED LAFLAMME, LIC

Ed celebrated his 46th year in the Green Industry in 2017, 30 years owning his own business and 16 consulting and coaching landscape owners. He is a Landscape Industry Certified professional (LIC) and author of the nationally acclaimed book, *GREEN SIDE UP, Straight talk on growing and operating a profitable landscaping business!* (available on CD's), and knows about hard work.

With $700 borrowed in 1971 from his mother, Ed bought two mowers and began his landscaping business servicing clients out of the trunk of his car. Nine years later he sold the residential segment of his business and concentrated his energies on the commercial and industrial sectors. He set his sights on the mother of all commercial contracts: General Electric's World Headquarters, located in Fairfield, Connecticut. In 1985, he was awarded their business; his first multi-million dollar account. With GE on his customer list he was unstoppable.

Over the next 10 years he acquired maintenance contracts for Xerox, ABB, Olin Chemical, GE Capital, Travelers Insurance, Bristol Myers, GTE, GenRe, Phillips Medical and many more. By this time between his landscaping and snow services, his company was the largest landscape maintenance contractor in Connecticut. In 1998, Laflamme Services, Inc. was listed as one of the top 100 revenue-generating landscaping companies in America by *Lawn & Landscape* magazine. In 1999, Laflamme sold his company to Landcare USA.

Today, Ed is an author, professional speaker, consultant/coach and mentor to "green industry" owners nationwide. In 2007, he formed The Harvest Group with his long-time friend Bill Arman where he uses his unique "one-on-one consulting" to act as a silent partner, helping his clients' businesses thrive and grow as a result of his personal mentoring. He and Bill along with the Harvest team speak both nationally and internationally doing business in 5 countries and 45 states.

Ed lives in Wilton, Connecticut, with his wife and two teenage sons.

ed@harvestlandscapeconsulting.com • 203-858-4696